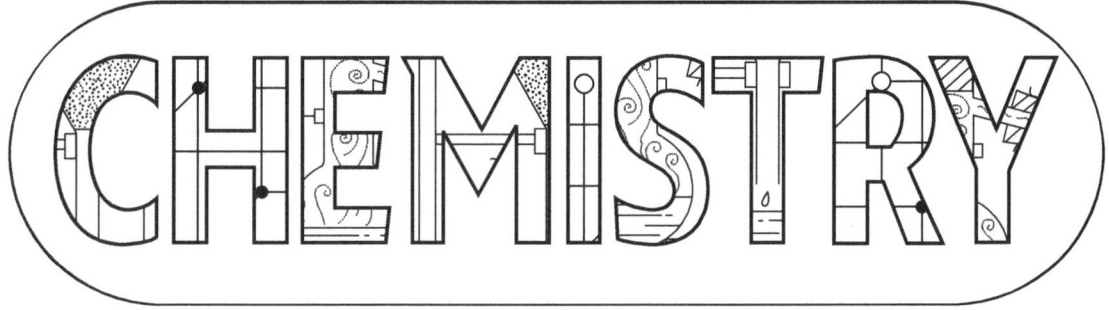

Revision Guide for CSEC® Examinations

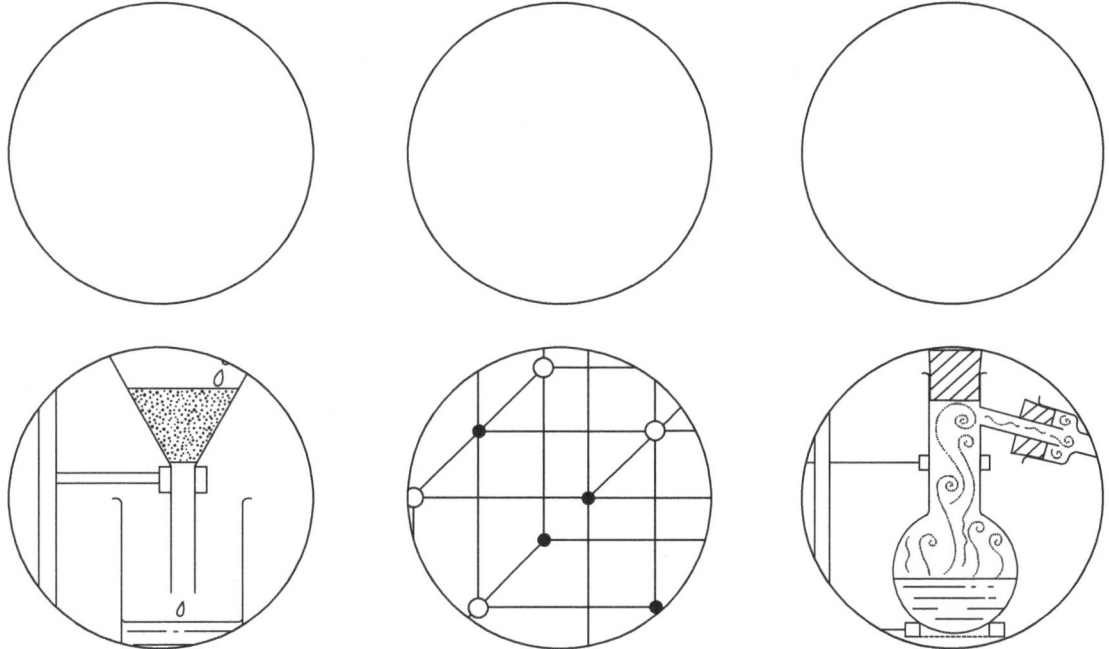

Compton Mahase and Mark Morris

CAMBRIDGE
UNIVERSITY PRESS

University Printing House, Cambridge CB2 8BS, United Kingdom

One Liberty Plaza, 20th Floor, New York, NY 10006, USA

477 Williamstown Road, Port Melbourne, VIC 3207, Australia

4843/24, 2nd Floor, Ansari Road, Daryaganj, Delhi – 110002, India

79 Anson Road, #06–04/06, Singapore 079906

Cambridge University Press is part of the University of Cambridge.

It furthers the University's mission by disseminating knowledge in the pursuit of education, learning and research at the highest international levels of excellence.

Information on this title: education.cambridge.org

© Cambridge University Press 2007

This publication is in copyright. Subject to statutory exception and to the provisions of relevant collective licensing agreements, no reproduction of any part may take place without the written permission of Cambridge University Press.

First published 1988
Second edition 2007
20 19 18 17 16 15 14 13 12 11 10 9 8

Printed in Great Britain by CPI Group (UK) Ltd, Croydon CR0 4YY

A catalogue record for this publication is available from the British Library

ISBN-13 978-0-521-69296-0 Paperback
ISBN-10 0-521-69296-2 Paperback

Typesetter: DTP Impressions, Cape Town
Illustrator: Karen Ahlschläger
Proofreader: Bridget Farham

Cambridge University Press has no responsibility for the persistence or accuracy of URLs for external or third-party internet websites referred to in this publication, and does not guarantee that any content on such websites is, or will remain, accurate or appropriate. Information regarding prices, travel timetables and other factual information given in this work is correct at the time of first printing but Cambridge University Press does not guarantee the accuracy of such information thereafter.

CSEC is a registered trademark of the Caribbean Examinations Council (CXC).

'Chemistry Revision Guide for CSEC® Examinations' is an independent publication and has not been authorised, sponsored, or otherwise approved by the Caribbean Examinations Council.

Contents

How to revise for the Chemistry CSEC® examination iv
Periodic table v
1 States of matter 1
2 Separation of mixtures 3
3 Atomic structure 5
4 Ionic combination 7
5 Covalent combination 9
6 Structure and properties of some solids 11
7 Periodic table – I 13
8 Periodic table – II 15
9 Acids and bases 17
10 Salts 19
11 Gas laws and the mole concept 21
12 Chemical formulae and equations 23
13 Volumetric analysis 27
14 Calculations involving volumetric analysis 30
15 Electrochemistry 32
16 Electrochemical and reactivity series 34
17 Electrolysis 37
18 Calculations involving electrolysis 40
19 Energy 42
20 Chemical energetics 43
21 Equilibria 45
22 Rate of reaction 47
23 Metals and non-metals 49
24 Extraction and uses of metals 51
25 Chemistry of some non-metals 53
26 Water 55
27 Some industrial processes 57
28 Preparation and identification of gases 59
29 Nitrogen cycle, carbon dioxide cycle and pollution 62
30 Qualitative analysis 64
31 Alkanes 66
32 Alkenes 69
33 Alcohols 71
34 Natural and synthetic macromolecules 74
Answers to questions 77
Appendix: Measurement 79

How to revise for the Chemistry CSEC® examination

Step 1 Syllabus and past examination papers

Ensure that you have a copy of the current syllabus as well as past examination papers. Look at the syllabus while you study and also work through the past examination papers. This will ensure that you cover all areas of the syllabus effectively while studying. You can get the syllabus and past examination papers from your local examination office, or at your school.

Step 2 Revise

Start revising early! Don't wait until just before the examination to start studying. Draw up a revision plan that covers all aspects of the syllabus a few weeks before the examination. Make sure that you allow yourself enough time to study each section well. Follow your revision plan so that you do not need to learn too much just before the examination.

The revision process should be active. You should write down definitions, equations and key points from your textbook or from memory. You can then use your shortened notes to help you study.

Pretend that you are writing an actual examination and work through the past examination papers. Once you have finished, refer to your notes and textbook to make sure your answers are correct.

Avoid studying late (or all night!) before the examinations, or else you will be tired when writing the examination. Do, however, get up early enough so that you can get to the examination room on time and have enough time to settle down.

Step 3 Read the questions carefully

Make sure that you understand each question and what is expected of you. Then answer the question as directly as possible. This may sound obvious, but many students lose marks by not reading carefully enough. For example, if you are asked to **name** a substance, and you give the **formula** as an answer, you will not earn any points.

Also avoid writing too much. Don't write everything you know about a topic if that is not what you were asked to do. Give only the information asked for. The examiner will only award you marks if you answer what has been asked for.

All the best for the upcoming examinations!

Periodic table

Group																	
I	II											III	IV	V	VI	VII	0
					¹H Hydrogen												⁴He 2 Helium
⁷Li 3 Lithium	⁹Be 4 Beryllium											¹¹B 5 Boron	¹²C 6 Carbon	¹⁴N 7 Nitrogen	¹⁶O 8 Oxygen	¹⁹F 9 Fluorine	²⁰Ne 10 Neon
²³Na 11 Sodium	²⁴Mg 12 Magnesium											²⁷Al 13 Aluminium	²⁸Si 14 Silicon	³¹P 15 Phosphorus	³²S 16 Sulphur	³⁵·⁵Cl 17 Chlorine	⁴⁰Ar 18 Argon
³⁹K 19 Potassium	⁴⁰Ca 20 Calcium	⁴⁵Sc 21 Scandium	⁴⁸Ti 22 Titanium	⁵¹V 23 Vanadium	⁵²Cr 24 Chromium	⁵⁵Mn 25 Manganese	⁵⁶Fe 26 Iron	⁵⁹Co 27 Cobalt	⁵⁹Ni 28 Nickel	⁶⁴Cu 29 Copper	⁶⁵Zn 30 Zinc	⁷⁰Ga 31 Gallium	⁷³Ge 32 Germanium	⁷⁵As 33 Arsenic	⁷⁹Se 34 Selenium	⁸⁰Br 35 Bromine	⁸⁴Kr 36 Krypton
⁸⁵Rb 37 Rubidium	⁸⁸Sr 38 Strontium	⁸⁹Y 39 Yttrium	⁹¹Zr 40 Zirconium	⁹³Nb 41 Niobium	⁹⁶Mo 42 Molybdenum	Tc 43 Technetium	¹⁰¹Ru 44 Ruthenium	¹⁰³Rh 45 Rhodium	¹⁰⁶Pd 46 Palladium	¹⁰⁸Ag 47 Silver	¹¹²Cd 48 Cadmium	¹¹⁵In 49 Indium	¹¹⁹Sn 50 Tin	¹²²Sb 51 Antimony	¹²⁸Te 52 Tellurium	¹²⁷I 53 Iodine	¹³¹Xe 54 Xenon
¹³³Cs 55 Caesium	¹³⁷Ba 56 Barium	¹³⁹La* 57 Lanthanum	¹⁷⁸Hf 72 Hafnium	¹⁸¹Ta 73 Tantalum	¹⁸⁴W 74 Tungsten	¹⁸⁶Re 75 Rhenium	¹⁹⁰Os 76 Osmium	¹⁹²Ir 77 Iridium	¹⁹⁵Pt 78 Platinum	¹⁹⁷Au 79 Gold	²⁰¹Hg 80 Mercury	²⁰⁴Tl 81 Thallium	²⁰⁷Pb 82 Lead	²⁰⁹Bi 83 Bismuth	Po 84 Polonium	At 85 Astatine	Rn 86 Radon
Fr 87 Francium	²²⁶Ra 88 Radium	²²⁷Ac† 89 Actinium															

* 58–71 Lanthanum series
† 90–103 Actinium series

140 Ce 58 Cerium	141 Pr 59 Praseodymium	144 Nd 60 Neodymium	Pm 61 Promethium	150 Sm 62 Samarium	152 Eu 63 Europium	157 Gd 64 Gadolinium	159 Tb 65 Terbium	162 Dy 66 Dysprosium	165 Ho 67 Holmium	167 Er 68 Erbium	169 Tm 69 Thulium	173 Yb 70 Ytterbium	175 Lu 71 Lutetium
232 Th 90 Thorium	Pa 91 Protactinium	238 U 92 Uranium	Np 93 Neptunium	Pu 94 Plutonium	Am 95 Americium	Cm 96 Curium	Bk 97 Berkelium	Cf 98 Californium	Es 99 Einsteinium	Fm 100 Fermium	Md 101 Mendelevium	No 102 Nobelium	Lr 103 Lawrencium

Key

$_b^a X$

a = relative atomic mass
X = atomic symbol
b = atomic number

number of moles of atoms = $\dfrac{\text{mass of element/g}}{\text{relative atomic mass } (A_r)}$ number of moles of substance = $\dfrac{\text{mass of substance/g}}{\text{relative molecular mass } (M_r)}$

The volume of one mole of any gas is 24 dm³ (litres) at room temperature and pressure (r.t.p.)

1 States of matter

There are three states of matter – solid, liquid and gas. For example, water can exist as solid ice, liquid water or as steam, which is a gas.

Many substances can be converted to a different state depending on the temperature and pressure. Some solid substances may decompose before they are converted to a liquid.

The names of the different changes of state are shown below:

$$\text{solid} \underset{\text{freezing}}{\overset{\text{melting}}{\rightleftharpoons}} \text{liquid} \underset{\text{condensation}}{\overset{\text{evaporation}}{\rightleftharpoons}} \text{gas}$$

A liquid can be converted to its vapour by evaporation or by boiling. Evaporation can take place at any temperature and pressure. But a liquid boils at a specific temperature depending on the pressure. For example, water boils at 100 °C when the atmospheric pressure is 760 mmHg.

Nature of matter

Matter is made up of particles. The following section provides evidence to support this theory.

Diffusion

A crystal of potassium manganate (VII) is placed at the bottom of a gas jar to which water is gently added. After a short time the whole solution will be coloured purple because the potassium manganate (VII) particles move upwards and spread throughout the liquid. This is known as **diffusion**. Similarly, if a few drops of bromine liquid are placed at the bottom of a gas jar and the gas jar is covered, the whole gas jar will soon be filled with bromine vapour. The bromine vapour diffuses upwards, although it is heavier than air.

Different gases diffuse at different rates, as demonstrated by the following experiment.

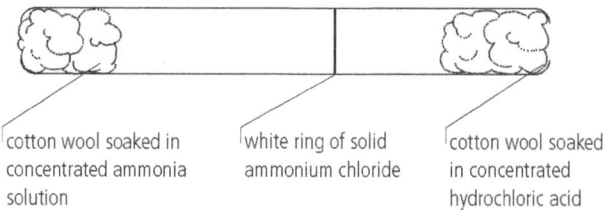

A white ring of ammonium chloride forms where the two gases meet. The experiment shows that not only do gases diffuse, but they do so at different rates. Which gas particles move faster? Why do you say so?

Brownian motion

Observation of brightly illuminated smoke particles in a small glass container will show the particles moving with a haphazard kind of movement. This same kind of movement was observed by the botanist Robert Brown as he observed pollen dust on water. These jerky, haphazard movements were caused by particles in the air or water colliding with the particles of smoke or pollen dust. This type of movement is called **Brownian motion**.

Osmosis

A sugar solution (about 15%) is placed in a thistle funnel covered with a Cellophane membrane. This is then placed in a beaker of water as shown below. The level of the solution in the thistle funnel rises. This is due to water particles passing through the membrane into the thistle funnel. No sugar particles pass into the beaker. The membrane is said to be semi-permeable. It allows solvent particles to pass through, to dilute a solution on the other side. This is known as **osmosis**. The same effect will be observed if a sugar solution of weaker concentration (10%) is placed in the beaker in place of the water. The process continues until the concentrations of both solutions are equal.

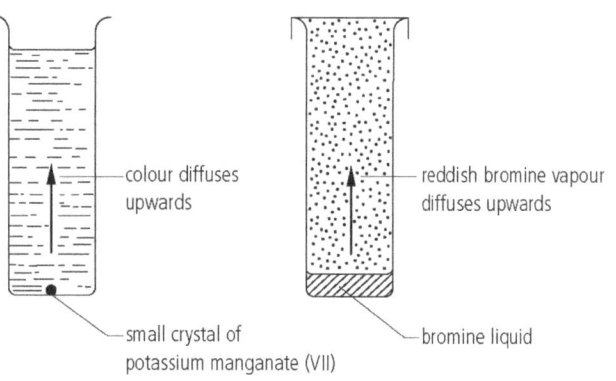

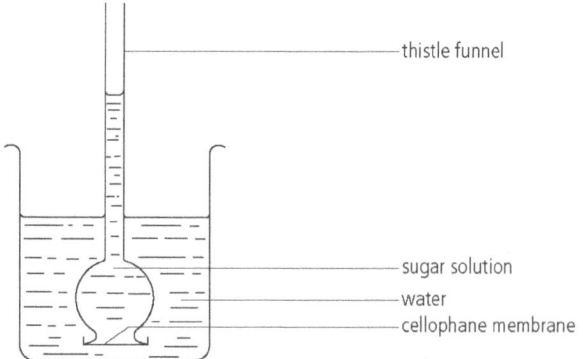

Dilution

A small crystal of potassium manganate (VII) is dissolved in a test tube of water. One-tenth of this solution is placed in another test tube which is filled with water and stirred. This process can be repeated many times before the colour of the manganate (VII) disappears. The solution is coloured because of the presence of particles of potassium manganate (VII). The fact that the solution retains a colour although diluted thousands of times suggests that the one crystal of potassium manganate (VII) must be made up of many tiny particles. (See Chapter 3 for an idea of the size of particles in matter.)

Arrangement of particles in solids, liquids and gases

In a solid, the particles are close to each other with strong forces of attraction between them. The particles are capable of small to-and-fro movements, called vibrational motion.

In a liquid, the forces of attraction are weaker than in a solid, hence they are further apart and capable of greater movement – haphazard movement called Brownian motion.

In a gas, there is little or no attraction between the particles, which are relatively further apart than in a liquid. These particles move at rapid speeds, thus possessing greater energy than those in a liquid.

Sublimation is when a solid goes directly to the gaseous state without passing through a liquid state. On cooling, the gas is also converted directly to a solid. Examples are iodine, ammonium chloride and dry ice.

Questions

1. Put in decreasing order the average energy that the particles in a solid, liquid and gas will possess.
2. 1 g of potassium manganate (VII) is dissolved to make 100 cm³ of the solution. 10 cm³ of this solution is placed in another beaker and the solution is made up to 100 cm³. This process can be repeated nine more times before the colour of the manganate (VII) becomes very faint. Assuming that the faint colour of the manganate (VII) must be caused by at least one particle of potassium manganate (VII), calculate the least number of particles that must be present in the 1 g.
3. One experiment that is frequently used to estimate the size of particles in a substance is the oil layer experiment. In one such experiment, a solution containing 0.1 cm³ of oleic acid in 1 dm³ of solution was used. One drop of this solution was placed on water in a trough. The water was sprinkled with a fine powder such as **lycopodium powder**.
   The area occupied by the oil film was estimated to be about 15 cm². 50 drops of the acid solution had a volume of 2.5 cm³.
   a Find the volume of one drop of the acid solution.
   b Find the volume of oleic acid in one drop of solution.
   c Assuming that the layer is a monomolecular layer, find the thickness of the layer giving the thickness of one molecule of oleic acid.
4. A beaker filled with hydrogen gas is placed over a porous pot containing carbon monoxide gas as shown in the diagram below. What will happen to the water level at X. Why?

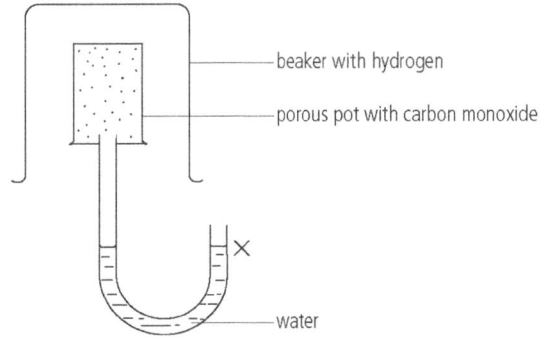

5. This question concerns the following table.

Substance	Melting point (°C)	Boiling point (°C)
A	−20	350
B	−285	−183
C	800	1 400
D	190	180
E	0	100
F	−7	59

a Which substance(s) will be solid(s) at room temperature (25 °C)?
b Which substance(s) will have fast-moving particles at room temperature?
c Which substance(s) will sublime when heated?
d Which substance will be liquid over the widest range of temperatures?
e Which substance(s) will be liquid(s) at room temperature?
f Which substance(s) will completely fill a container?

2 Separation of mixtures

Substances occur naturally as mixtures. Thus, knowing how to obtain pure substances from mixtures is of great importance. For example, common salt (sodium chloride) occurs naturally as rock salt with sand being the major impurity. The salt can be separated from the sand to obtain a pure salt substance.

A **pure substance** is one that contains particles of that substance only, for example, pure sodium chloride contains crystals of sodium chloride only. The addition of any other substance causes it to become a mixture.

Methods of separation

Filtration

Filtration is used to separate a solid from a liquid in which the solid is not dissolved. This is called a **suspension**, for example, sand and water or undissolved zinc in a solution of zinc sulphate.

A filter funnel and filter paper are used to separate the solid and liquid, as shown below.

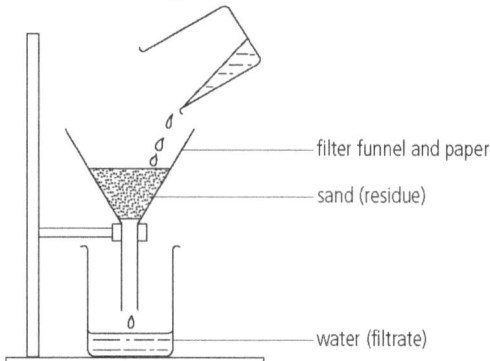

Evaporation

Evaporation is used to obtain a solid from a solution of a solid and a liquid. For example, if you have a solution of sodium chloride and water, you can recover the sodium chloride by evaporating all the water from the solution leaving the less volatile sodium chloride behind. This process is limited to salts that will not decompose on heating, and those that do not need water for the crystals to form. Such crystals can be obtained from a solution by crystallisation.

Note: In a **solution** the solid is dissolved in the liquid.

Crystallisation

At any particular temperature, only a fixed amount of a solid can dissolve in a fixed amount of liquid. This is normally referred to as the **solubility** of the solid.

Consider a solution of solid in a liquid in which almost all of the liquid is evaporated. The little liquid that is left cannot dissolve all of the solid. As the solution is cooled, the solid therefore starts to separate from the solution as crystals. The crystals can then be obtained by filtration.

Simple distillation

This is a process by which pure water can be obtained from impure water.

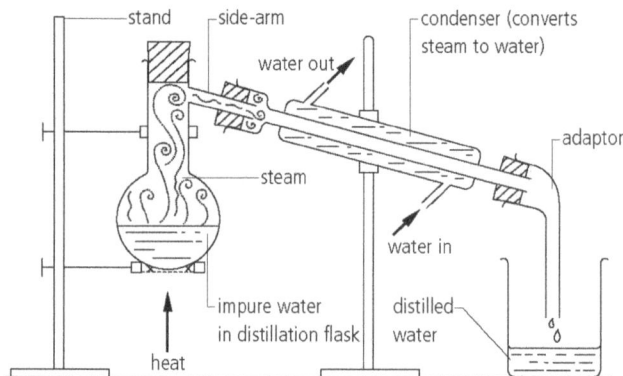

The less volatile solid impurities are left in the distillation flask.

Separation of miscible and immiscible liquids

Fractional distillation

This process is used to separate mixtures of miscible liquids, i.e. liquids that dissolve in each other. The most popular example is the separation of a mixture of ethanol and water.

Ethanol normally boils at around 78 °C and water at 100 °C. If a 40 : 60 mixture is heated in a distillation flask, the first distillate collected will be much richer in alcohol (about 70–80%). A better separation is normally obtained using a fractionating column (shown on page 4).

In the fractionating column, several distillations take place at the same time. As vapour ascends the column, it condenses to a liquid. Hot vapour ascends and redistills the condensed liquid driving it forward. This continues along the length of the column. Each time the liquid is redistilled, the vapour driven forward is richer in the more volatile (low-boiling) component. In this case, a 95% : 5% separation can be obtained by this method.

Oil refineries use this method to separate petroleum into fractions such as gasoline, kerosene or gas oil.

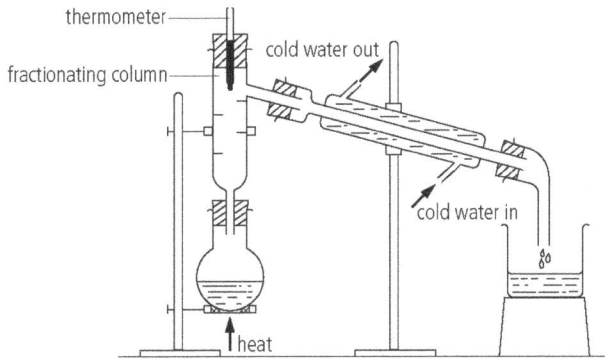

Separation of immiscible pairs of liquids – by separating funnel

A pair of immiscible liquids, i.e. liquids that do not dissolve in each other, such as oil and water, can be separated using a separating funnel. This is a funnel with a stopcock at the end.

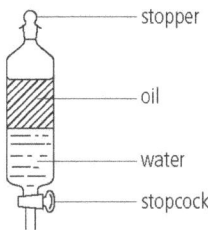

Oil and water do not dissolve in each other so will occupy separate layers when mixed, with the lighter substance (oil) floating on top of the water. The mixture is placed in a separating funnel and the water is run off first, followed by the oil. It is often very difficult to allow all of the water to run out leaving the oil behind. Usually, most of the water is allowed to run out and then the tap is turned off. The small quantity of water remaining is then run out along with a little of the oil, into a separate container. The oil can then be safely run out.

Other methods of separation

Paper chromatography

This is used for separating mixtures of dyes, for example, ink. Several methods can be used, as illustrated in the next column. All the methods involve putting a spot of a concentrated solution of the substance on the paper and allowing it to dry.

The different dyes separate out because each dye moves at a different rate on the paper. This is due to two factors: (a) solubility in the solvent: the more soluble the dye is in the solvent, the faster its rate of movement, and (b) the attraction of the dye for the paper: the greater the attraction, the slower the movement. Paper chromatography is also used to identify and separate mixtures of, for example, amino acids or sugars.

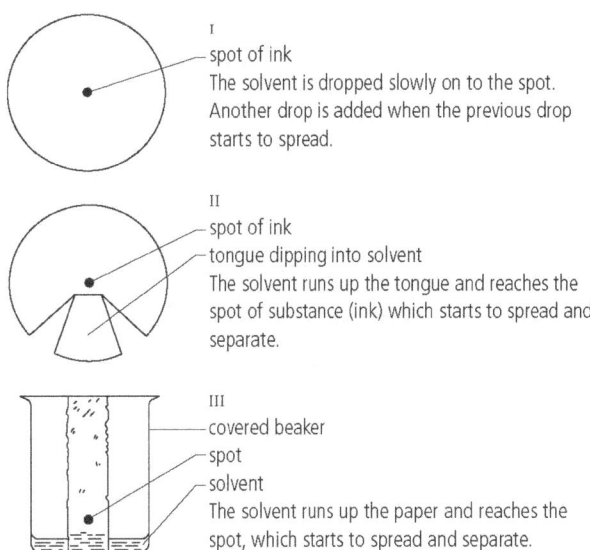

Solvent extraction

This process is mainly used to separate organic substances from aqueous solutions. An organic solvent (nearly always ether) is used to extract the organic compound. Once the ether is added, the organic substance dissolves in it. There will be two layers which can be separated using a separating funnel. The organic substance can then be obtained by distillation and the solvent can also be recovered. This process is used in the manufacture of penicillin.

Solvent extraction can also be used for extracting vegetable oils from substances such as nuts or soya beans. The nuts are crushed and the solvent is used to extract the oils. The mixture can then be filtered and distilled, separating the oil from the solvent, which is recovered.

Sublimation

This is used to separate a mixture of two solids, only one of which sublimes, for example, ammonium chloride and sodium chloride. The mixture is heated causing the ammonium chloride to sublime and leaving the sodium chloride behind. The ammonium chloride cools to a solid and can be recovered. Iodine can be purified in this way.

Questions

1. Water is added to a mixture of copper(II) sulphate crystals and copper(II) oxide. The mixture is warmed, stirred and then filtered.
    a. Explain what will be achieved by the above operations.
    b. Why is the mixture stirred and warmed?
    c. On filtering, what will be (i) the residue, and (ii) the filtrate?
    d. Can any crystals be obtained from the filtrate? If so, how?
2. List three differences between colloids and suspensions.

3 Atomic structure

An atom of an element consists of three particles:

Particles	Mass/atomic mass unit (a.m.u.)	Charge
Protons	1	+
Neutrons	1	0
Electrons	1/1850	−

The protons and neutrons are in the nucleus at the centre of the atom. The electrons orbit the nucleus at distances representing different energy levels. Each energy level is referred to as a shell.

The atomic number of an element is the number of protons in the nucleus of the atom.

The mass number is the sum of the protons and neutrons in the nucleus of an atom of the element.

In any atom, the number of protons is equal to the number of electrons. Consider the notation $^{23}_{11}Na$. Na is the symbol of the element sodium. The upper figure represents the mass number (23). The lower figure represents the atomic number (11). Thus, in an atom of sodium, there will be:
- protons: atomic number (11)
- electrons: atomic number (11)
- neutrons: mass number − atomic number (23 − 11).

The number of neutrons is obtained by subtracting the atomic number from the mass number. The sodium atom can be represented simply like this.

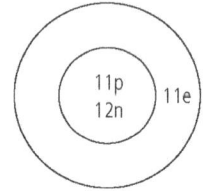

Arrangement of electrons in atoms

The electrons are arranged in shells around the nucleus. Each shell represents a different energy level. The first shell is the K shell, followed by the L shell, M shell, etc. The maximum number of electrons in a shell is given by the formula $2n^2$, where n is the number of the shell. For example:

Shell	Maximum number of electrons
K shell, $n = 1$	$2n^2 = 2 \times 1^2 = 2$
L shell, $n = 2$	$2n^2 = 2 \times 2^2 = 8$
M shell, $n = 3$	$2n^2 = 2 \times 3^2 = 18$

Consider the sodium atom with 11 electrons. These electrons will be arranged as follows: 2 in the first shell, 8 in the second and 1 in the third. This can be represented as 2)8)1 and is referred to as the **electronic configuration**. The sodium atom can be represented like this:

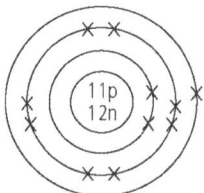

In working out electronic configurations the following rules must be observed:
a A shell cannot accommodate more than its maximum electrons, but may have less.
b The outermost shell of an atom can never have more that eight electrons. If such a situation arises, electrons in excess of eight are put into a new shell.

For example: potassium has an atomic number of 19, therefore the atom will have 19 electrons. It should have been possible to write the electronic configuration as 2)8)9. However, this would violate rule b. The electronic configuration is therefore 2)8)8)1.

Isotopy

Very often an atom may have more than one type of atom, for example, $^{35}_{17}Cl$ and $^{37}_{17}Cl$. Notice that the atomic number is the same in both cases but the mass numbers are different. Work out the number of protons, neutrons and electrons in each of these atoms. As you can see, they have the same number of protons and electrons but a different number of neutrons. This phenomenon is known as **isotopy** and the different types of atoms are isotopes of the element. These isotopes are not present in the same proportion. In a sample of chlorine, there are 75% of $^{35}_{17}Cl$ atoms to 25% of $^{37}_{17}Cl$ atoms. Thus, the relative atomic mass of chlorine will be:

$$\frac{(75 \times 35) + (25 \times 37)}{100}$$

= 35.5, taking 100 atoms into account.

Because isotopes have the same number of electrons arranged in the same way, they will show similar chemical behaviour.

Absolute mass and relative mass

The absolute mass of a single atom is too low for it to be weighed accurately. For example, the mass of a hydrogen atom is approximately:

$$\frac{1}{6 \times 10^{23}} \text{ g}$$

Masses of atoms are therefore compared with a standard atom. This mass is referred to as the **relative atomic mass**. The standard first chosen was hydrogen. Nowadays the standard used is carbon-12 which is assigned a mass of 12 atomic mass units. Atoms of all other elements are compared to that of carbon-12. Thus, if an atom is twice as heavy as a carbon atom, it will have a relative atomic mass of 24.

Questions

1. a How many protons, electrons and neutrons are present in each of the following elements?
   i $^{40}_{20}Ca$
   ii $^{40}_{18}Ar$
   iii $^{1}_{1}H$
   iv $^{2}_{1}H$

   b Draw diagrams to represent the calcium and argon atoms.

2. Protons, neutrons and electrons are passed through an electric field, as shown in the diagram.

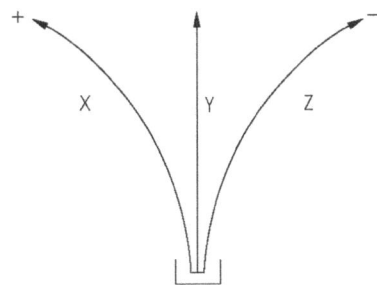

   Which letters represent the protons, neutrons and electrons respectively?

3. a X and Y are two isotopes of the same element. Complete the following table.

Isotope	X	Y
Number of protons	48	
Number of electrons		
Number of neutrons	48	50

   b A sample of the element contains 70% of isotope X and 30% of isotope Y. What is the relative atomic mass of the element?

4. The table below contains information about various atoms.

Atom	Number of protons	Number of neutrons
A	17	18
B	22	26
C	17	20
D	22	28
E	28	31

   a Which pairs of atoms are isotopes of the same element?
   b What is the mass number of atom B?
   c What is the electronic configuration of atom C?
   d Which element will have the electronic configuration 2)8)16)2?

5. The number of protons in the atom $^{A}_{Z}M$ is:
   A Z B A − Z C A D Z − A

6. The number of protons in the atom $^{A}_{Z}M$ is:
   A Z B A − Z C A D Z − A

7. The number of neutrons in the atom $^{A}_{Z}M$ is:
   A Z B A − Z C A D Z − A

8. The electronic configuration of an element with atomic number 19 and mass number 20 will be:
   A 2)8)9 B 2)8)8)1 C 2)8)8)2 D 2)8)19)8)3

9. Two isotopes of an element are present in equal proportions. If the mass numbers of the isotopes are 88 and 90 respectively, what is the relative atomic mass of the element?
   A 88.5 B 89 C 89.5 D 90

10. Which of the following elements contain the same number of neutrons as $^{40}_{20}Ca$?
    A $^{20}_{10}Ne$ B $^{40}_{18}Ar$ C $^{27}_{13}Al$ D $^{39}_{19}K$

4 Ionic combination

The basic units of all substances are **elements**. An element is any substance which cannot be split up into simpler substances by any known chemical process. Elements combine with each other to form **compounds**. A compound is any substance formed when two or three elements are chemically combined.

Why and how do elements combine?

Helium, neon, argon, etc., the noble gases, are chemically inert, i.e. they are stable. All of them, except helium, have eight (an octet of) electrons in their outermost shell. It is this octet of electrons which makes these elements so stable. In the case of helium, which has only one shell, a duplet is enough to fill the shell and thus ensure stability. All elements try to attain this electronic stability, i.e. they try to attain the electronic configuration of the nearest inert gas. It is the electrons in atoms and their instability that are responsible for chemical reactivity. How they have this effect leads us to chemical combination.

Ionic or electrovalent combination

This type of combination takes place when a metal combines with a non-metal. Consider the elements sodium ($^{23}_{11}$Na) and chlorine ($^{35}_{17}$Cl). The electronic configuration of sodium is 2)8)1 and that of chlorine 2)8)7. Sodium needs to lose 1 electron to attain the electronic configuration of neon 2)8 whereas chlorine needs to gain 1 electron to attain the electronic configuration of argon 2)8)8. When the two elements react together, sodium gives an electron to chlorine which accepts it. Each atom has now attained electronic stability.

By losing an electron, sodium now has one more proton (+) than electron (−). Thus, the sodium atom is no longer neutral. It now has a positive charge, Na$^+$. A charged atom is called an **ion**. Chlorine now has one more electron than proton. It has therefore acquired a negative charge. Ions, because they are oppositely charged, attract each other by an electrostatic force of attraction. This electrostatic force of attraction is called an **ionic** or **electrovalent** bond.

In ionic compounds, the ions are arranged in cubes with negative ions surrounded by positive ions and vice versa. For example, in sodium chloride, each sodium ion is surrounded by six chloride ions and each chloride ion is surrounded by six sodium ions.

Before combination

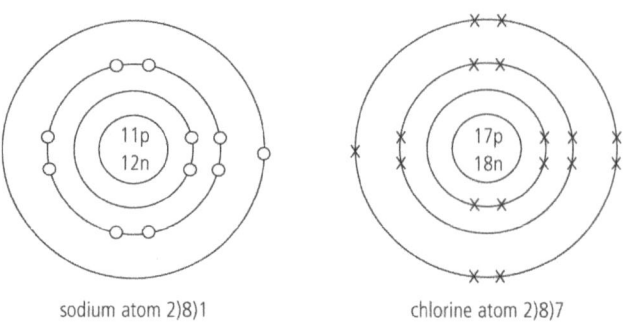

sodium atom 2)8)1   chlorine atom 2)8)7

After combination

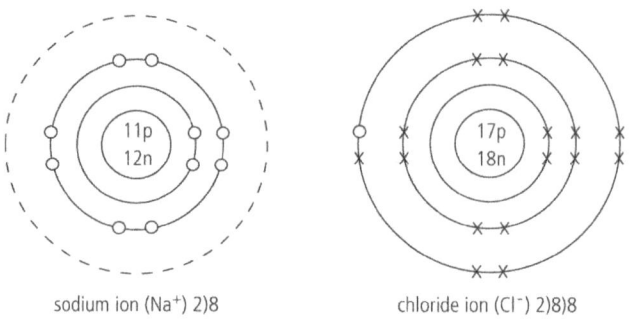

sodium ion (Na$^+$) 2)8   chloride ion (Cl$^-$) 2)8)8

If sodium 2)8)1 combines with sulphur 2)8)6, two sodium atoms will combine with one atom of sulphur.
Before combination:
   Na 2)8)1   Na 2)8)1   S 2)8)6
After combination:
   Na$^+$ 2)8   Na$^+$ 2)8   S^{2-} 2)8)8
How will magnesium $^{24}_{12}$Mg combine with chlorine $^{37}_{17}$Cl? Write your answer as shown above.

Properties of ionic compounds

1. Ionic compounds normally have a giant structure of oppositely charged ions. These ions strongly attract each other. As a result, all ionic compounds are solids with high melting points, high boiling points and high heats of vaporisation.
2. Ionic compounds do not conduct electricity when solid but do so in aqueous solution or when molten (liquid). Ions move only slightly in the solid as they are strongly attracted to each other. In the liquid

state, or in aqueous solution, the forces of attraction between the ions are broken down by heat and the solvent respectively. The **ions** become more mobile and are able to conduct an electric current.
3 It is an adage in chemistry that 'like dissolves like'. Thus, ionic compounds are soluble in polar solvents like water and insoluble in non-polar solvents like gasoline or methylbenzene (toluene).

Ionic equations

In many equations there are ions which remain unchanged in state or in valency across an equation. These are called **spectator ions**. If these are removed from an equation, an ionic equation is formed.

Here are the steps to write an ionic equation:

Step 1 Write the balanced chemical equation:
$Pb(NO_3)_2(aq) + 2NaCl(aq) \rightarrow PbCl_2(s) + 2NaNO_3(aq)$

Step 2 Break up the compound into ions:
$Pb^{2+}(aq) + 2NO_3^-(aq) + 2Na^+(aq) + 2Cl^-(aq) \rightarrow$
$Pb^{2+}(s) + 2Cl^-(s) + 2Na^+(aq) + 2NO_3^-(aq)$

Step 3 Eliminate the ions which are not changed:
$Pb^{2+}(aq) + 2\cancel{NO_3^-}(aq) + 2\cancel{Na^+}(aq) + 2Cl^-(aq) \rightarrow$
$Pb^{2+}(s) + 2Cl^-(s) + 2\cancel{Na^+}(aq) + 2\cancel{NO_3^-}(aq)$

Step 4 Rewrite the equation with whatever is left:
$Pb^{2+}(aq) + 2Cl^-(aq) \rightarrow PbCl_2(s)$

Tips for writing ionic equations
1 The element always has a valency of 0.
2 Covalent compounds cannot be broken into, for example, H_2O, CO_2 and NH_3.
3 Two ions that come from the same compound on the same side of the equation are rejoined in the final ionic equation.

Types of chemical reactions
1 A **combined reaction** is when two reactions combine to give one product, for example:
   a $S(s) + O_2(g) \rightarrow SO_2(g)$
   b $Na_2O(s) + CO_2(g) \rightarrow Na_2CO_3(s)$
2 When some substances are heated, they can break down or decompose. This break down is called **decomposition**, for example:
   $2NaNO_3(s) \rightarrow 2NaNO_2(s) + O_2(g)$
3 Neutralisation occurs when acids and bases react until their pH is exactly 7 or neutral, for example:
   $HCl(aq) + NaOH(aq) \rightarrow NaCl(aq) + H_2O(l)$
4 A metal or non-metal may displace another from its salts. This is called **displacement**, for example:
   a $Zn(s) + CuSO_4(aq) \rightarrow ZnSO_4(aq) + Cu(s)$
   b $Cl_2(g) + 2KI(aq) \rightarrow 2KCl(aq) + I_2(aq)$

5 When salt solutions are mixed together, they exchange ions. This is known as **double displacement**, for example:
   $2NaNO_3(aq) + ZnSO_4(aq) \rightarrow Zn(NO_3)(aq) + Na_2SO_4(aq)$

Questions
1 Draw diagrams to show the combination between:
   a sodium and oxygen
   b magnesium and chlorine.
2 Use the electronic configurations of the elements to write the formula of the following compounds:
   a lithium oxide   b sodium sulphate
   c magnesium oxide   d calcium chloride.
   In each case show the charges on the ions.
3 Complete the following table.

Element	Atomic number	Number of protons	Number of electrons	Charge on ions
A	17		18	
B		20		B^{2+}
C			18	C^{2-}
D		1		D$^+$
E		8	10	

4 Consider the following diagram.

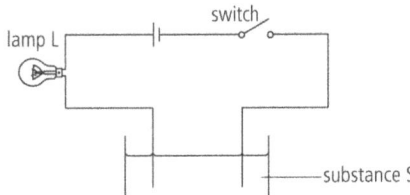

When the switch is closed, the lamp L lights up if substance S is aqueous or molten magnesium chloride. When S is solid magnesium chloride, the lamp does not light up. Explain this.

5 Why is it that ionic compounds have high melting and boiling points?

6 During ionic combination:
   A a non-metal donates electrons to a non-metal
   B a metal accepts electrons from a non-metal
   C a metal loses its valency electrons to a non-metal
   D a metal donates one electron to a non-metal.

7 During ionic combination, atoms:
   I try to attain the electronic structure of the nearest noble gas
   II seek to obtain a stable electronic structure by losing or gaining electrons
   III share electrons to attain a stable electronic structure.
   Choose the correct answer:
   A I, II and III   **C** II and III only
   B I and II only   **D** I only

5 Covalent combination

This type of combination takes place mainly between non-metals. Consider the $_1^1H$ (hydrogen) and $_{17}^{35}Cl$ (chlorine) atoms.

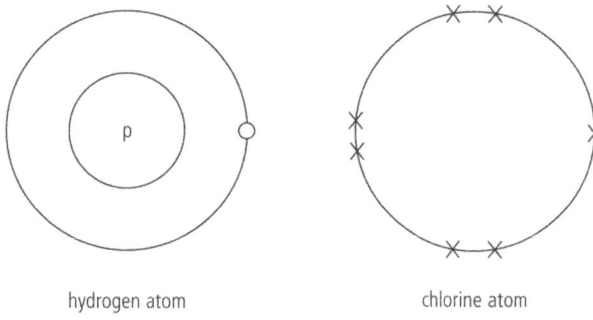

hydrogen atom   chlorine atom

Hydrogen needs one electron to complete its shell and attain the electronic structure of helium. Chlorine also needs one electron to complete its octet and attain the electronic structure of argon. Chlorine and hydrogen do this by sharing electrons. The hydrogen electron orbits around its own nucleus, and also around the chlorine nucleus, thus completing the octet for chlorine. Chlorine, in turn, allows one of its electrons to orbit around its own nucleus and also the hydrogen nucleus. The hydrogen duplet is thus completed. The two atoms are sharing electrons to attain stability. This sharing of electrons can be represented as follows.

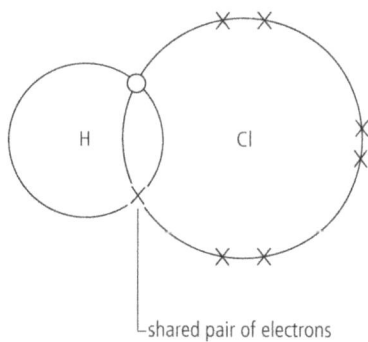

shared pair of electrons

This shared pair of electrons forms a covalent bond. Consider the combination between phosphorus and chlorine.

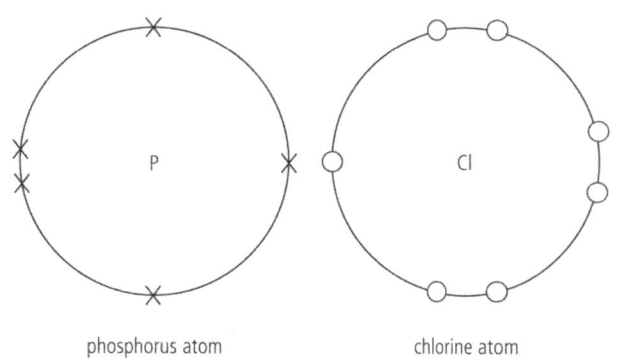

phosphorus atom   chlorine atom

Phosphorus needs three more electrons to complete the octet and chlorine needs one electron to complete its octet. Phosphorus will therefore have to share one electron with each of three chlorine atoms, which will in turn share one electron each with the phosphorus atoms, for example:

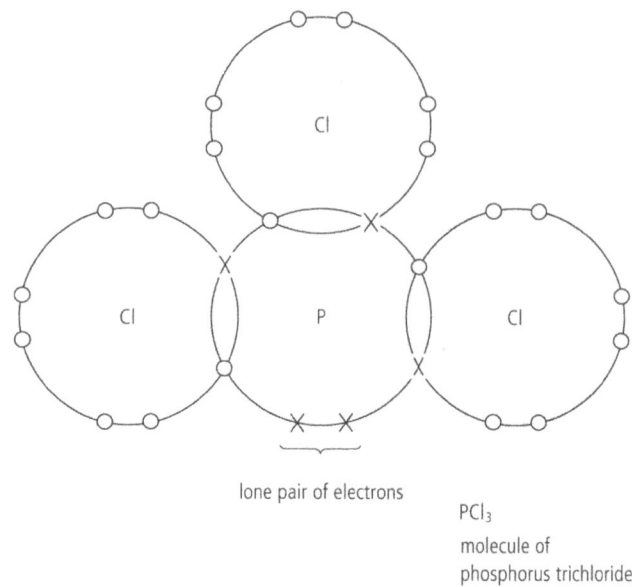

lone pair of electrons

PCl_3 molecule of phosphorus trichloride

Thus, three covalent bonds are produced.

Covalent bonds

The simplest example to illustrate the concept of a covalent bond is the hydrogen molecule. A hydrogen molecule consists of two hydrogen atoms in which the two valence electrons are shared between the two atoms. This diagram shows covalent bonds in a hydrogen molecule.

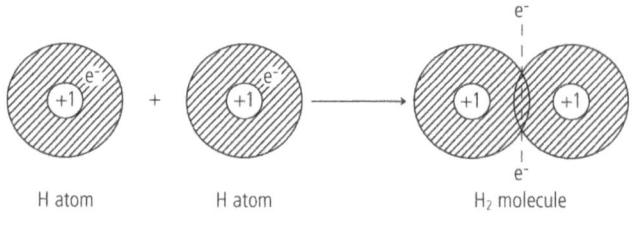

H atom   H atom H_2 molecule

The shaded region on each atom is known as an **orbital** — it is the region in which the electrons will be found. When the orbitals overlap, the two electrons, one from each atom, are attracted to the two nuclei at the same time, thereby forming a single covalent bond.

It is important to note the following:
1. The atoms do not lose or gain the electrons.
2. Covalent bonds are electrostatic in nature.
3. The chemical bond in the hydrogen molecule forms because each of the two electrons is attached to two protons simultaneously. The bonding electrons are often said to be shared by two nuclei.
4. Substances such as hydrogen, in which the bonding between the atoms in the molecule is covalent, are called **covalent molecular substances**. The covalent bond is also found in a network of solids such as diamond and graphite (see Chapter 6). However, by sharing the two electrons, the atoms in the hydrogen molecule have achieved the electron configuration of the noble gas atom, helium.

A simpler way of representing the bonding in the hydrogen molecule is as follows.

$$H\text{———}H \quad \text{or} \quad H:H$$
$$\text{I} \qquad\qquad\qquad\quad \text{II}$$

Note that in I the line represents a shaded pair of electrons, while in II the hydrogen bond can be expressed as an electron pair on the electron dot diagram.

Lone pairs are the valence electrons, which are not involved in the covalent bonds.

Examples of lone pairs:

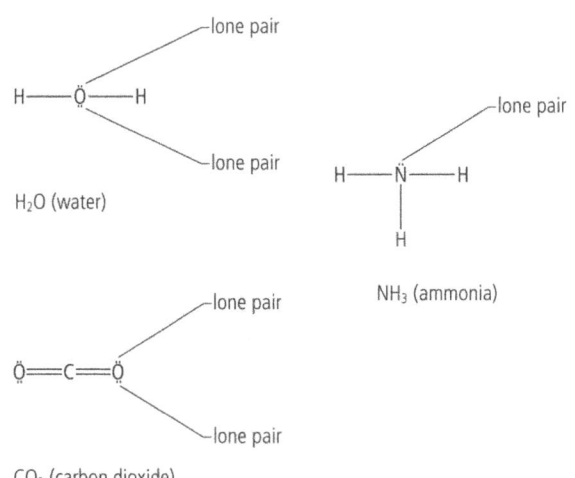

H_2O (water)

NH_3 (ammonia)

CO_2 (carbon dioxide)

The difference between ionic compounds and covalent molecular substances can be set out as follows.

Ionic compounds	Covalent molecular compounds
Generally crystalline solids, for example, salts.	Generally liquids or gases.
High melting and boiling point – non-volatile.	Low melting and boiling point – volatile.
Electrolytes.	Non-electrolytes.
Generally soluble in water, but insoluble in organic solvents.	Generally soluble in organic solvents, but insoluble in water.
Bonding is non-directional.	Bonding is highly directional.
Reactions are fast.	Reactions are often slow.

Questions

1. a Use electronic configurations to write formulae for compounds formed between:
    i carbon and chlorine
    ii nitrogen and hydrogen
    iii sulphur and chlorine.
   b Draw diagrams to illustrate the combination in the above compounds.
2. What kind of combination (if any) will be expected to take place between the following?
   a sodium and oxygen
   b carbon and oxygen
   c phosphorus and oxygen
   d phosphorus and chlorine
   e hydrogen and chlorine
   f sodium and sulphur
   g sodium and magnesium
   h helium and oxygen
3. Are these chlorides formed by ionic or covalent combination?
   A is a gas at room temperature.
   B is a high melting solid at room temperature.
   C has a boiling point of −1 °C.
   D is a gas at room temperature that conducts electricity when dissolved in water.
   E is insoluble in water, but conducts electricity when molten.
4. Covalent combination:
   A usually takes place between a metal and a non-metal
   B occurs because metals are unstable
   C usually takes place between two non-metals
   D takes place by the transference of electrons from one non-metal to another.
5. Covalent compounds are usually gases or liquids at room temperature because:
   A the covalent bonds are weak
   B there is little attraction between the molecules
   C the atoms are closely attached to each other
   D the particles are capable of rapid movement.

6 Structure and properties of some solids

The physical properties of solids are closely related to their structures. Consider the structures and properties of three solids – diamond, graphite and sodium chloride.

Diamond

Diamond is an allotrope of carbon. The element carbon has four electrons in the outermost shell. Each carbon atom can therefore form four covalent bonds. In diamond, each carbon atom is covalently bonded to four other atoms. The four covalent bonds are directed towards the corner of a tetrahedron. In this way, diamond is made up of a three-dimensional network of carbon atoms, each linked tetrahedrally to four other carbon atoms. The crystal formed is a giant molecule.

Graphite

Graphite is another allotrope of carbon. This allotrope consists of hexagonal layers of carbon atoms lying on each other.

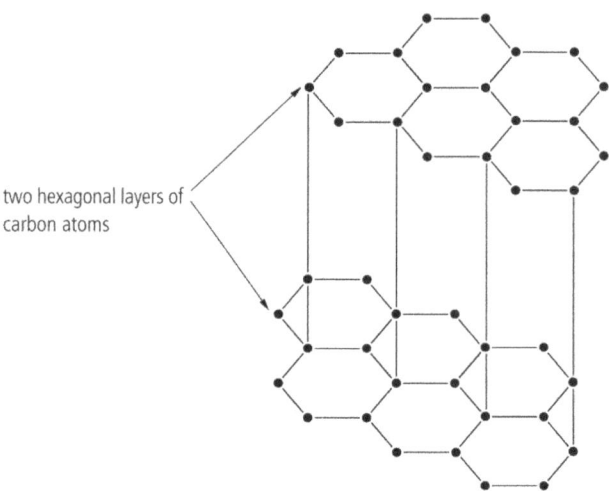

one flat layer of carbon atoms in a hexagonal arrangement

two hexagonal layers of carbon atoms

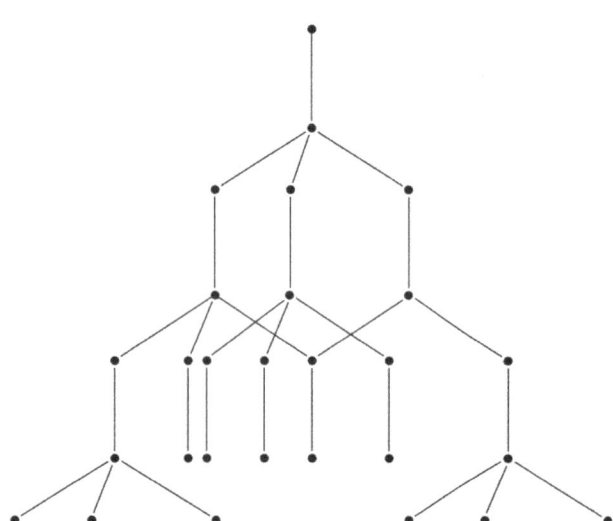

Because of this strong, three-dimensional structure, diamond is the hardest natural substance known to humans. It can be used to cut glass and drill rocks, etc. Since all the electrons are used up in covalent bonding, it cannot conduct electricity. The strong forces of attraction, due to the continued covalent bonding throughout the lattice, cause diamond to have a very high melting point. Diamond is a compact substance as can be deduced from its high density. It is capable of diffracting light to a great extent. This gives it a great lustre and it is therefore very valuable as jewellery.

Each layer is attracted to the other by weak forces called **Van der Waal's forces**. These layers can slide on each other giving graphite lubricating properties. Thus, graphite can be used along with clay to make the 'lead' in lead pencils. Each carbon atom is bonded to three others within the layer and therefore has a free mobile electron. This makes graphite a good conductor of electricity and it can therefore be used for electrodes. Graphite also has a very high melting point of about 3 500 °C. Because of its refractory nature, it can be used to make crucibles for molten metals.

Sodium chloride

Sodium chloride is an ionic compound containing sodium ions and chloride ions in a cubic lattice. It is therefore an ionic crystal.

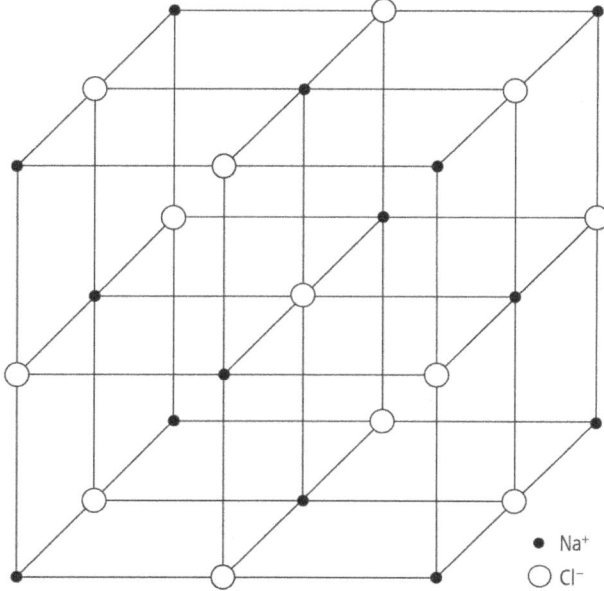

In the unit cell, the first layer consists of sodium ions at the corners and face and chloride ions on the edges. The second layer consists of chloride ions on the corners and face and sodium ions on the edges. The third is as the first. The cell is therefore made up of inter-penetrating face-centred cubes of chloride and sodium ions.

The solid has a high melting point of about 800 °C. This is due to the strong forces of attraction within the cubic lattice. The forces of attraction must be broken down before the solid melts. The ions are capable only of small vibrational movement within the solid. Hence it can only conduct electricity when molten. In the molten state, the ions have greater mobility due to decreased forces of attraction. It can also conduct electricity in aqueous solution as the water considerably reduces the forces of attraction between the ions making them more mobile.

This table summarises the properties of diamond, graphite and sodium chloride.

Properties	Diamond	Graphite	Sodium chloride
Melting point	Very high	Very high	Very high
Hardness	Hardest	Soft	Very hard
Lubricating power	Poor	Good	Poor
Electricity conductivity	Poor	Very good	Good only when dissolved

Questions

1. Graphite is capable of conducting electricity because it:
   A is made up of hexagonal layers of carbon atoms
   B has electrons that are mobile
   C consists of positively charged particles
   D is an allotrope of carbon.
2. Diamond can be described as a:
   A giant molecule
   B simple covalent molecule
   C giant ionic compound
   D metallic crystal.
3. Which of the following properties of diamond is not true?
   A It has great lustre.
   B Its density is high.
   C It is a good conductor of electricity.
   D It is the hardest natural substance known.
4. Sodium chloride can conduct electricity when molten, but not when solid because:
   A it ionises when heated
   B its ions become mobile when the compound is melted
   C it contains free electrons in the molten state
   D it is a covalent compound.
5. What is responsible for the lubricating properties of graphite?
6. Diamond is an extremely hard, shiny substance, but graphite is a soft, shiny substance. Explain why this is so.
7. The table below gives some properties of three substances, A–C.

Substance	Melting point (°C)	Boiling point (°C)	Ability to conduct electricity	
			When solid	In aqueous solution
A	800	1 464	Nil	Good
B	3 700	Sublimes	Good	Insoluble
C	3 550	4 830	Nil	Insoluble

a Which substance could be
  i graphite
  ii diamond
  iii sodium chloride?
b Explain how you made your choice.

7 Periodic table – I

A brief history of the development of the periodic table

The earliest classification of elements was in the broad categories of metals and non-metals. However, chemists tried to arrange elements in smaller groups. Below is a brief history of the development of the periodic table.

Early nineteenth century

Dobereiner arranged elements in triads. The three elements arranged in the triad had similar properties. When the elements were arranged in order of atomic mass, the properties of the middle element were intermediate between those of the other two elements.

Two such triads were:
a lithium, sodium, potassium
b chlorine, bromine, iodine.

1866

John Newlands proposed the Law of Octaves. He suggested that, when the elements were arranged in order of atomic mass, the eighth element had properties of the first one. His paper was not well received. He failed because (a) not all elements were known and the discovery of one more would upset his order, and (b) many elements with different properties were grouped together.

1868

Lothan Meyer plotted physical properties (boiling point, melting point, density, atomic volume) against atomic mass. He found that the curves had repeating patterns and that elements with similar properties appeared on similar points on the different parts of the curves. Hence he found that physical properties were a periodic function of atomic mass.

1869

Dmitri Mendeléev arranged the then known elements in a table known as the periodic table. The elements were arranged in order of atomic mass. Elements with similar properties re-occurred at regular intervals and fell into the same vertical columns which were called **groups**. The horizontal rows were called **periods**.

Mendeléev's table was successful because he left gaps in his table to ensure that elements with similar properties fell into the same vertical groups. He suggested that the gaps represented missing elements and even predicted their properties. These elements were later discovered. When elements occurring in the same group had different properties they were placed in sub-groups. For example, of the elements (Na, K, Cu, Rb, Ag) Na, K and Rb were placed on the left-hand side of the column and Cu and Ag on the right.

Today

In the modern periodic table the elements are arranged in order of atomic number. The properties of elements are dependent on their atomic numbers. The other departure from Mendeléev's table is the arrangement of the transition elements in horizontal rows. Four of the groups are called by special names:

Group I   alkali metals
Group II   alkaline earth metals
Group VII   halogens
Group 0   noble gases

Trends and relationships in the periodic table

1 Elements in the same group have the same number of electrons in the outermost shell. The valencies of the elements are the group numbers up to Group IV. After Group IV, the valency is either the group number, or more usually 8 minus the group number. Thus, the valency of elements in Group II is 2 and that of elements in Group VI is also 2.

2 Electropositivity increases down a group, and across a period from right to left. Electronegativity increases up a group, and across a period from left to right.

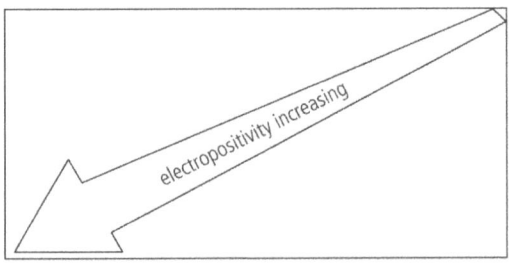

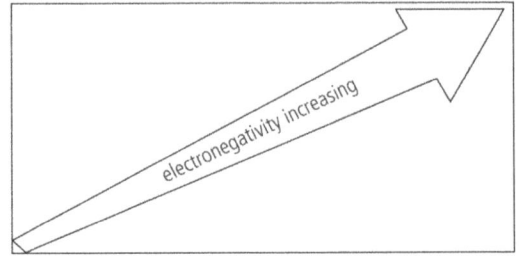

3 As a result of (2), reactivity increases down a metallic group and up a non-metallic group. Potassium will be more reactive than sodium, whereas chlorine will be more reactive than bromine.

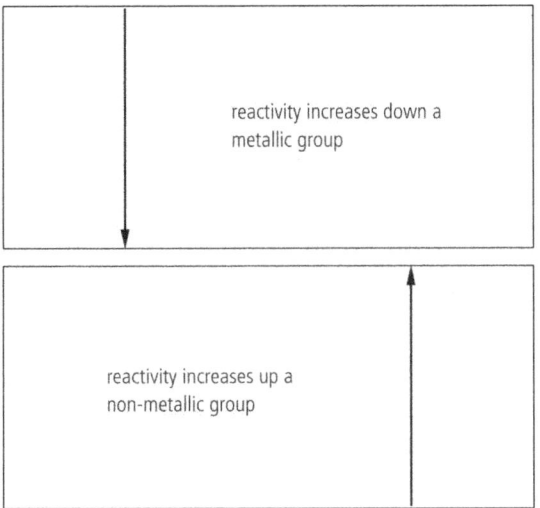

4 The diagonal or step (see periodic table) separates metals from non-metals. Some elements near the diagonal are called **metalloids** (elements having properties similar to both metals and non-metals), for example, boron, carbon, germanium and silicon.

Questions

1 What are the two broadest categories that elements can be divided into? Is this a satisfactory classification? Explain.
2 What was the basis for Newlands' classification? Why did the chemists of his day ridicule his classification?
3 Mendeléev's classification was widely accepted by his colleagues. Why? What was the basis for his classification?
4 Which of the following elements will be expected to have similar electropositivity?
lithium, sodium, magnesium, calcium, beryllium, aluminium
5 For each of the following pairs of elements, state which one will generally be more reactive.
  a chlorine or bromine   c sulphur or oxygen
  b sodium or potassium   d calcium or magnesium
6 Element X is below potassium in Group I of the periodic table. X would be expected to:
  A have an insoluble hydroxide
  B be extremely reactive with cold water
  C have a carbonate that rapidly decomposes when heated
  D form a chloride with a low melting point.
7 Elements in the same group of the periodic table will be expected to have:
  I   the same valency
  II similar chemical properties
  III similar physical properties.
  A I, II and III   **C** II and III only
  B I and II only   **D** I only
8 Element Q is in period 4 of the periodic table. Q will:
  A have a valency of 4
  B be a metal
  C be a non-metal
  D have four electronic shells.

Periodic table (also see page v)

number of moles of atoms = $\dfrac{\text{mass of element/g}}{\text{relative atomic mass } (A_r)}$

number of moles of substance = $\dfrac{\text{mass of substance/g}}{\text{relative molecular mass } (M_r)}$

The volume of one mole of any gas is 24 dm³ (litres) at room temperature and pressure (r.t.p.)

8 Periodic table – II

Trends in Group II

Group II consists of the following elements: beryllium, magnesium, calcium, strontium, barium and radium. They all have two electrons in their outermost shell and so exhibit a valency of two, with a fixed oxidation state of +2.

All the metals react readily with oxygen when heated to form their respective oxides. The oxide of beryllium is covalent, but the oxides of the others are ionic.

The reaction with water increases in vigour as the group is descended. Thus, beryllium reacts with steam, magnesium reacts very slowly with cold water, but readily with steam.

$Mg(s) + H_2O(g) \rightarrow MgO(s) + H_2(g)$

Calcium reacts readily with cold water. The reaction increases in vigour for the others down the group.

$Ca(s) + 2H_2O(l) \rightarrow Ca(OH)_2(aq) + H_2(g)$

These oxides are all alkaline. The metals from magnesium downwards will all react with dilute acids to form their respective salts and will liberate hydrogen gas in the process. The reactions with sulphuric acid between the metals below magnesium will stop after a while because insoluble sulphate forms around the metal. This prevents the acids from attacking the metals.

Ionisation of the metals takes place more easily as the group is descended and this accounts for the increase in reactivity in that direction. The solubilities of the hydroxides increase as the group is descended, whereas the solubilities of the sulphates decrease as the group is descended.

Important facts about Group II:
1. The elements are reducing agents.
2. The elements have high melting points due to the metallic structure.
3. All elements in Group II react with water, oxygen and acids.
4. The reactivity of the elements in Group II, increases down the group.
5. In Group II, the oxides and hydroxides of the elements are basic.
6. The elements in Group II (except Be) react with acids to give a salt and hydrogen gas.
7. The ionisation energy decreases to form positive ions.
8. In Group II the compounds formed, conduct electricity when molten.

Trends in Group VII (the halogens)

The main elements in Group VII are fluorine, chlorine, bromine and iodine. They each have seven electrons in their outermost shell. The one electron needed to complete the octet can be obtained through ionic bonding with metals or through covalent bonding with non-metals. These elements show a marked change (gradation) in both physical and chemical properties as the group is descended.

Element	State at 25 °C	Colour
Fluorine	Gas	Yellowish
Chlorine	Gas	Greenish-yellow
Bromine	Liquid	Red
Iodine	Solid	Black

The increase in melting point can be attributed to greater inter-molecular attractions as the group is descended, this being due to a greater number of charged particles. The change in reactivity can be shown by reacting the halogens with aqueous halide compounds of the other elements below them. So, chlorine will displace bromine and iodine from bromides and iodides respectively, and bromine will displace iodine from iodides:

$Cl_2(aq) + 2KBr(aq) \rightarrow 2KCl(aq) + Br_2(aq)$
$Br_2(aq) + 2KI(aq) \rightarrow 2KBr(aq) + I_2(aq)$

This also demonstrates their strengths as oxidising agents F > Cl > Br > I. Fluorine, the most electronegative, will be the strongest oxidising agent (acceptor of electrons) and iodine the weakest. Fluorine, chlorine and bromine can oxidise iron(II) ions to iron(III) ions but iodine cannot. Fluorine will also react most vigorously with metals and iodine the least.

We can therefore say that:
1. The reactivity increases up Group VII.
2. Group VII elements form compounds by gaining or sharing electrons.
3. The melting point increases down the group as the atomic number increases.
4. The solubility in water increases down the group. Chlorine will react with water to form soluble products.
5. Group VII elements have seven electrons in the outer shell.

Trends across Periods 2 and 3

Period 2

Elements	Li	Be	B	C	N	O	F	Ne
Type of element	Metals	Metalloid	←	Non-metals			→	
Formula of oxide	Li$_2$O	BeO	B$_2$O$_3$	CO$_2$	NO$_2$	O$_2$	F$_2$O	None
Bonding in oxide	Ionic	←		Covalent			→	
Nature of oxide	Basic	←	Amphoteric	←	Acidic		→	

Period 3

Elements	Na	Mg	Al	Si	P	S	Cl	Ar
Type of element	← Metals →			← Non-metals →				
Formula of oxide	Na$_2$O	MgO	Al$_2$O$_3$	SiO$_2$	P$_4$O$_6$	SO$_2$	Cl$_2$O	None
Bonding in oxide	←Ionic→		Ionic with some covalent characteristics	←Covalent→				
Nature of oxide	Basic		Amphoteric	← Acidic →				
Formula of chloride	NaCl	MgCl$_2$	AlCl$_3$	SiCl$_4$	PCl$_3$	S$_2$Cl$_2$	Cl$_2$	None
Bonding in chloride	←Ionic→		Coordinate covalent	← Covalent →				
Reaction of chloride with water	Dissolves			Hydrolysed to give acidic solutions				
Electrical conductivity	Good conductors			Poor conductors				

The above table illustrates the change from metallic to non-metallic characteristics as a period is traversed from left to right. Hence, bonding in oxides and chlorides changes from ionic to covalent. The nature of the oxides changes from basic through amphoteric to acidic. The metals are also good conductors of electricity, whereas the non-metals are poor conductors.

Important facts about Period 3:
1. In Period 3 there is a shift across the period from metallic to non-metallic character.
2. In Period 3 the oxides of the elements can be basic, amphoteric and acidic.
3. The lower ionisation energies of the larger atoms result in the formation of positive ions.

Questions

Questions 1–12 refer to the shortened periodic table shown at the top of the next column. Letters represent various elements.

	I	II	III	IV	V	VI	VII	0
1	A							P
2	B	G		K			L	Q
3	C	H	J				M	R
4	D	I					N	
5	E						O	
6	F							

1. Which element will react the most vigorously with cold water?
2. Which of the elements B–D will form a carbonate that dissolves sparingly in water?
3. Which of the elements B–D will form a hydroxide which will be decomposed by the heat of a flame?
4. Which elements will have a valency of 2?
5. Which element in Group II will have:
   a. the most soluble sulphate?
   b. the most soluble hydroxide?
6. Which element will have four electrons in the outermost shell?
7. Which element forms an amphoteric oxide?
8. Which elements form neutral oxides?
9. Which element has the lowest density?
10. Which will be the most reactive element in Group I?
11. Which element has one form that conducts electricity and another that does not?
12. Which is the most reactive element in Group VII?
13. This question concerns the oxides across Period 3 of the complete periodic table shown on page 14.
    a. Which oxides in the period are ionic?
    b. Which oxides in the period are covalent?
    c. What is formed when each of the oxides of the elements in Period 3 is dissolved in water? What effect does each solution have on litmus?
    d. One of the oxides in the period is insoluble in water but is considered to be an acidic oxide. State which oxide it is, and explain why it is classified as an acidic oxide.
14. What type(s) of bonding is/are present in the chlorides as Period 3 is traversed from left to right? What effect will water have on each chloride?
15. YCl$_2$ is a chloride which is a volatile liquid at room temperature. In which group will Y be found?
    A I   **B** II   **C** V   **D** VI
16. Barium is in the same group of the periodic table as calcium. Barium will be expected to:
    A have an insoluble hydroxide
    B react readily with cold water
    C have a soluble sulphate
    D form a covalent chloride.
17. Elements X, Y and Z are in the same period of the periodic table. X forms a covalent oxide, Y an ionic, and Z an amphoteric oxide. The correct order in the periodic table will be:
    A XYZ   **B** ZYX   **C** YZX   **D** XY

9 Acids and bases

An acid is any substance which, in aqueous solution, produces hydroxonium ions (H_3O^+) as the only positive ions.

$HCl(g) + H_2O(l) \rightarrow H_3O^+(aq) + Cl^-(aq)$

$H_3O^+(aq)$ is very often represented simply as H^+.

An **acid anhydride** is a non-metallic oxide which dissolves in water to form an acid.

pH scale

The pH scale measures how acidic or how alkaline a substance is.

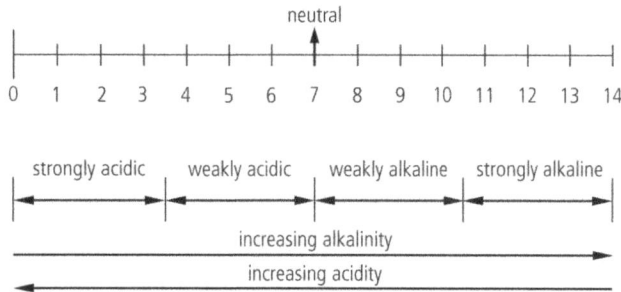

Determination of the approximate pH of a substance

Moist pH paper is placed in or against the substance. The colour of the pH paper is then matched with the colours on a pH chart, which would have the pH written on the colour.

The pH of soil can be similarly determined. The soil is shaken up with distilled water and a few drops of universal indicator added. The colour of the resulting solution is matched to a colour on a colour chart as above. Universal indicator (or pH paper) gives a different colour for each unit change of pH. Its neutral colour is green.

Strengths of acids

Some acids are almost completely ionised and are known as **strong** acids, for example, hydrochloric, sulphuric and nitric acids. These acids will have a very low pH. Other acids are ionised only to a small extent. These are known as **weak** acids, for example, ethanoic acid and carbonic acid. Weak acids exist mainly as molecules in aqueous solution. They have a high pH, but it is lower than 7.

Unless an acid ionises, it will not show acidic behaviour. The acid must have a solvent that is willing to accept a proton if it is to ionise.

Water is a proton acceptor so hydrogen chloride behaves as an acid in water. When hydrogen chloride is dissolved in methylbenzene (toluene) (organic solvent), it remains un-ionised as methylbenzene is not a proton acceptor. Hydrogen chloride in methylbenzene will therefore *not* act as an acid.

Basicity of acids

The basicity of an acid is the number of moles of hydrogen ions produced per mole of the acid. For example:

$HCl(aq) \rightarrow H^+(aq) + Cl^-(aq)$
$HNO_3(aq) \rightarrow H^+(aq) + NO_3^-(aq)$
$CH_3COOH(aq) \rightarrow H^+(aq) + CH_3COO^-(aq)$

are all monobasic (have a basicity of one), whereas

$H_2SO_4 \rightarrow 2H^+(aq) + SO_4^{2-}(aq)$

is dibasic (has a basicity of two).

Bases

A base is anything that combines with hydrogen ions, for example:

$Cl^-(aq) + H^+(aq) \rightarrow HCl(aq)$
weak base   strong acid

$OH^-(aq) + H^+(aq) \rightarrow H_2O(l)$
strong base   very weak acid

$H_2O(l) + H^+(aq) \rightarrow H_3O^+(aq)$
very weak base   strong acid

The base forms an acid when it combines with hydrogen ions. This is known as a **conjugate acid–base pair**. If the acid formed is weak, the base is strong, and vice versa.

Basic oxides or hydroxides

A basic oxide (hydroxide) is a metallic oxide (hydroxide) which contains oxide ions (O^{2-}) (hydroxide ions, OH^-) and will react with an acid to form a salt and water only, for example:

$Mg^{2+}O^{2-}(s) + 2HCl(aq) \rightarrow MgCl_2(aq) + H_2O(l)$

or ionically

$Mg^{2+}O^{2-} + 2H^+ \rightarrow Mg^{2+}(aq) + H_2O(l)$

Alkalis

An alkali is a soluble metallic hydroxide, for example, NaOH, Ca(OH)$_2$.

Reactions of acids

With metals

The metals from potassium to iron in the reactivity series (see Chapter 18) react with acids to liberate hydrogen gas, for example:

$Zn(s) + H_2SO_4(aq) \rightarrow ZnSO_4(aq) + H_2(g)$

or ionically

$Zn(s) + 2H^+(aq) \rightarrow Zn^{2+}(aq) + H_2(g)$

Nitric acid, being an oxidising agent, produces water instead of hydrogen gas except when very dilute nitric acid reacts with magnesium.

With carbonates and hydrogen carbonates

All carbonates react with dilute acids to liberate carbon dioxide. A salt and water are also formed, for example:

$CaCO_3(s) + 2HCl(aq) \rightarrow CaCl_2(aq) + CO_2(g) + H_2O(l)$

or ionically

$CO_3^{2-}(s) + 2H^+(aq) \rightarrow H_2O(l) + CO_2(g)$

If the salt formed is insoluble, the reaction will cease after a short while. This is because the insoluble salt will form a layer around the carbonate that the acid cannot penetrate, for example:

$CaCO_3(s) + H_2SO_4(aq) \rightarrow CaSO_4(s) + H_2O(l) + CO_2(g)$

The calcium sulphate will form an impenetrable layer around the carbonate. Hydrogen carbonates also react with acids to form a salt, water and carbon dioxide.

$HCO_3^-(s) + H^+(aq) \rightarrow CO_2(g) + H_2O(l)$

Bases

Bases and alkalis react with acids to form a salt and water only, for example:

$NaOH(aq) + HCl(aq) \rightarrow NaCl(aq) + H_2O(l)$

or ionically

$OH^-(aq) + H^+(aq) \rightarrow H_2O(l)$

or $CuO(s) + H_2SO_4(aq) \rightarrow CuSO_4(aq) + H_2O(l)$

This kind of reaction is called **neutralisation**. In the reaction, hydrogen ions from the acid combine with hydroxide ions from the alkali to form molecules of water. A salt is also formed in the process.

Reaction of bases with ammonium salts

If a mixture of an ammonium salt and a base is warmed, ammonia gas is produced. This gas can be recognised by its characteristic odour (smelling salts) and by the fact that it turns litmus blue.

$NH_4^+(s) + OH^-(s) \rightarrow NH_3(g) + H_2O(l)$

Questions

1. An acid:
   I liberates carbon dioxide from carbonates
   II liberates hydrogen from all elements
   III contains hydroxonium ions (H$_3$O$^+$) in aqueous solution.
   A I, II and III   **C** I and III only
   B I and II only   **D** I only

2. A solution of pH 2 will be expected to:
   A turn moist red litmus blue
   B neutralise a solution of pH 6
   C liberate hydrogen gas from zinc
   D liberate ammonia gas from an ammonium compound.

3. A weak acid is one that is:
   A very dilute
   B ionised to a small extent
   C ionised to a large extent
   D unable to liberate hydrogen gas from metals.

4. Which of the following carbonates will not readily react with dilute sulphuric acid?
   A calcium carbonate   **C** sodium carbonate
   B copper carbonate   **D** magnesium carbonate

5. Which of the following acids can form acid salts?
   A hydrochloric acid (HCl)
   B ethanoic acid (CH$_3$COOH)
   C sulphuric acid H$_2$SO$_4$
   D none of the above

6. a Complete the following table. X is a solution of hydrogen chloride in methylbenzene (toluene). Y is a solution of hydrogen chloride in water. Where there is no reaction write 'none'.

Substance	Solution X	Solution Y
Copper carbonate		
Litmus		
Zinc		
Lead		

b Explain the differences in behaviour between X and Y.

10 Salts

A salt is a substance formed by replacing all, or some, of the hydrogen ions in an acid, by a metal. The salt is an ionic compound formed between a metallic ion and the anion from the acid.

Types of salts

If some of the hydrogen ions are replaced, the salt is called an **acid salt**, for example, sodium hydrogen sulphate ($NaHSO_4$). Only some of the hydrogen ions in sulphuric acid have been replaced. Monobasic acids cannot form acid salts as all of the hydrogen ions will always be completely replaced by metals.

When all of the hydrogen ions are replaced by a metal, the salt is called **normal salt**, for example, sodium chloride (NaCl) and sodium sulphate (Na_2SO_4).

Basic salts

If a base or alkali reacts with an acid and only some of the hydroxide ions are replaced by the anions of the acid, the salt formed is called a **basic salt**, for example:

$$Mg(OH)_2(aq) + HCl(aq) \rightarrow Mg^{2+}OH^-Cl^-(aq) + H_2O(l)$$
$$\text{basic salt}$$

Methods of preparing salts

In describing methods of preparing salts, the following points should be taken into account:
a starting materials
b any special precautions to be taken
c the isolation and drying of the salt.

Precipitation

Insoluble salts can be obtained as a precipitate (an insoluble solid formed when a solution is reacted), for example the preparation of insoluble barium sulphate.

Starting materials	Method	Isolation
Barium nitrate or barium chloride and sulphuric acid or any soluble sulphate of approximately the same concentration.	Mix equal volumes (50 cm³) of each solution in a beaker. Barium sulphate will be obtained as a white precipitate: $Ba^{2+}(aq) + SO_4^{2-}(aq) \rightarrow BaSO_4(s)$.	The salt can be obtained by filtration as a precipitate which can then be washed with distilled water and dried.

It is important to remember that all common metallic nitrates are soluble.

By reacting a metal with an acid

Soluble salts can be prepared by using this method. This method is suitable for the metals from magnesium to iron in the reactivity series. Metals above magnesium will react too violently with dilute acid and those below iron will not displace hydrogen from dilute acids.

Magnesium sulphate:
$$Mg(s) + 2H^+(aq) \rightarrow MgSO_4(aq) + H_2(g)$$

Starting materials	Method	Isolation
Magnesium and dilute sulphuric acid.	Add pieces of magnesium to about 50 cm³ of dilute sulphuric acid in a beaker until reaction stops. This is to ensure that all the acid is neutralised. If this is not done, the acid will be concentrated when the salt is being crystallised.	The salt is isolated by crystallisation (see Chapter 2), washed with a little distilled water and dried.

Other methods of preparing soluble salts are by:
a reacting a carbonate with an acid
b reacting an alkali with an acid (neutralisation)
c reacting a basic oxide with an acid.

The method is basically the same as that described for magnesium sulphate, ensuring that the acid is completely neutralised by the other substance. For the neutralisation reaction, it would be better to start with known concentrations of acid and alkali and react from them in quantities that will exactly neutralise each other.

Direct combination

Salts can also be prepared by directly combining the elements in the salt, for example:
Iron(III) chloride can be prepared by combining iron and chlorine. (The same method can be used for aluminium(III) chloride.)

$$2Fe(s) + 3Cl_2(g) \rightarrow 2FeCl_3(g)$$

The following apparatus can be used.

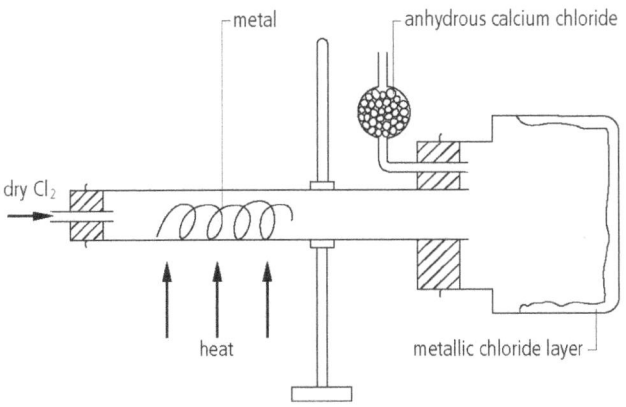

Solubility of salts

Salts have different solubility in water. The solubility of salts are determined by three factors:
a temperature
b a crystal lattice which is hard to break up when it releases energy
c the difference in the ions' size.

The table below shows how some elements react in water and acids.

Elements	Reaction in water	Reaction in acids
Lithium	Reacts slowly	Reacts violently
Sodium	Reacts vigorously	Reacts violently
Potassium	Reacts vigorously	Reacts violently
Calcium	Steady reaction	Reacts violently
Magnesium	Reacts slowly	Reacts faster
Caesium	Reacts more violently	Reacts faster

Salts which do not dissolve in water are: lead sulphate $PbSO_4$, calcium sulphate $CaSO_4$, lead chloride $PbCl_2$ and silver chloride $AgCl$. Beryllium does not react with water, but reacts rapidly with acids.

Remember: all nitrate and some chlorides are soluble in water. All sulphates are soluble in water, except $PbSO_4$, $BaSO_4$ and $CaSO_4$. All carbonates are insoluble in water, except sodium carbonate Na_2CO_3, potassium carbonate K_2CO_3 and ammonium carbonate $(NH_4)_2CO_3$. All bromides and iodides are soluble in water, except Ag and Pb salts. All hydroxides are insoluble in water, except NaOH and KOH. $Ba(OH)_2$ and $Ca(OH)_2$ are slightly soluble in water.

Salts of small anions increase in solubility because of the decreasing lattice dissociation. However, salts of large anions decrease in solubility because of their enthalpy of hydration.

Questions

1. Which of the following salts can be obtained by precipitation?
   I lead sulphate
   II lead(II) chloride
   III barium sulphate
   A I, II and III   **C** I and III only
   B I and II only   **D** II and III only

2. Which of the following are acid salts?
   I CH_3COONa
   II $NaHCO_3$
   III $KHSO_4$
   A I, II and III   **C** II and III only
   B I and II only   **D** III only

3. A normal salt is one that:
   A contains an anion that cannot ionise further to produce hydrogen ions
   B contains hydrogen atoms than can be replaced by a metal
   C contains no hydrogen atoms
   D is neither acidic or alkaline.

4. Which pair of substances will be unsuitable for the preparation of a metallic sulphate?
   A barium chloride and dilute sulphuric acid
   B sodium carbonate and dilute sulphuric acid
   C zinc and dilute sulphuric acid
   D calcium carbonate and dilute sulphuric acid.

5. Magnesium sulphate can be prepared by reacting magnesium with dilute sulphuric acid in a beaker. It is necessary to ensure that excess magnesium is used.
   a Write an ionic equation for the reaction.
   b Why should an excess of magnesium be used in the preparation?
   c How is the excess magnesium removed from the solution?
   d Describe how you would obtain a sample of magnesium sulphate from the above preparation.

6. Barium sulphate can be prepared by a precipitation reaction.
   a Name two pairs of substances that can be used to prepare barium sulphate.
   b Write an ionic equation for the reaction.
   c How is the barium sulphate separated from the solution?
   d What can be done to make sure that the sample of barium sulphate is reasonably pure?
   e Can barium sulphate be prepared by reacting barium with dilute sulphuric acid? Explain.

11 Gas laws and the mole concept

Avogadro's law
Avogadro's law states that equal volumes of all gases at the same temperature and pressure contain the same number of molecules. For example, if 100 cm^3 of hydrogen at standard temperature and pressure (s.t.p.) contains x molecules, then 100 cm^3 of oxygen at s.t.p. will also contain x molecules.

Application of Avogadro's law
It is known experimentally that 'one volume of hydrogen combines with one volume of chlorine to produce two volumes of hydrogen chloride', all volumes being measured at the same temperature and pressure.

If one volume of hydrogen contains x molecules then Avogadro's law enables us to rewrite the above statement as follows:

x molecules of hydrogen combine with x molecules of chlorine to produce $2x$ molecules of hydrogen chloride.

The one molecule of hydrogen combines with one molecule of chloride to produce two molecules of hydrogen chloride.

Avogadro's law therefore allows us to change from the easily measured volumes we use during experiments to molecules, which are the particles actually taking part in the reaction.

Guy-Lussac's law
Guy-Lussac's law states that when gases react, they do so in volumes which bear a simple whole number ratio to each other and also to the volumes of the products if gaseous; all volumes being measured at the same temperature and pressure. For example:
a one volume of hydrogen combines with one volume of chlorine to give two volumes of hydrogen chloride
b one volume of nitrogen combines with three volumes of hydrogen to give two volumes of ammonia.

Note: The total volume of reactants is not always the same as the total volume of products. The volume of products may be the same as, greater than, or less than, the volume of reactants.

Mole concept
The mole is a basic unit of mass in chemistry and is of great importance in quantitative work.

A mole is the amount of substance in grams that contains the same number of particles (atoms or molecules) as there are atoms in 12 g of carbon-12. 12 g of carbon-12 contains 6.02×10^{23} atoms of carbon. This number is known as the Avogadro constant.

2 g of hydrogen contains 6.02×10^{23} molecules of hydrogen.
1 mole of hydrogen is therefore 2 g.

32 g of oxygen contains 6.02×10^{23} molecules of oxygen.
1 mole of oxygen is therefore 32 g.

44 g of carbon dioxide contains 6.02×10^{23} molecules of carbon dioxide.
1 mole of carbon dioxide is therefore 44 g.

98 g of sulphuric acid contains 6.02×10^{23} molecules of sulphuric acid.
1 mole of sulphuric acid is therefore 98 g.

From the above it can be observed that one mole of a substance is its relative molecular mass expressed in grams.

For example, sodium hydroxide, NaOH, has a relative molecular mass (R.M.M.) of $23 + 16 + 1 = 40$.

One mole of sodium hydroxide is 40 g. Since sodium hydroxide is ionic, we cannot speak of it in terms of molecules. It would be more correct to describe it as an ion-pair or formula unit (Na$^+$OH$^-$); 40 g of sodium hydroxide will contain 6.02×10^{23} ion-pairs of sodium hydroxide.

One mole of a substance can also be described as its molar mass.

Molar volume
The volume occupied by 1 mole of a gas is called the molar volume. At standard temperature and pressure (s.t.p.), i.e. 0 °C and 760 mmHg pressure, the molar volume is 22.4 litres (dm^3). At room temperature and pressure (r.t.p.), i.e. 25 °C and 760 mmHg pressure, the molar volume is 24 litres (dm^3). For example:
- 2 g of hydrogen will occupy 22.4 ℓ at s.t.p.
- 2 g of hydrogen will occupy 24 ℓ at r.t.p.
- 44 g of carbon dioxide will occupy 24 ℓ at r.t.p.
- 24 ℓ of oxygen at r.t.p. will weigh 32 g.

It follows that the molar volume of any gas will contain 6.02×10^{23} molecules of the gas.

Sample calculations

1. How many molecules are there in 0.016 g of methane (CH_4)?

   The R.M.M. of methane is $12 + (4 \times 1) = 16$
   The molar mass of methane is 16 g
   16 g of methane contains 6.02×10^{23} molecules
   0.016 g of methane will contain:

   $$6.02 \times 10^{23} \times \frac{0.016}{16}$$

   $= 6.02 \times 10^{20}$ molecules

2. What volume will 2.2 g of carbon dioxide occupy at s.t.p. if C = 12 and O = 16?

   The R.M.M. of carbon dioxide CO_2
   $= 12 + (2 \times 16) = 44$
   1 mole of carbon dioxide is 44 g
   44 g of carbon dioxide at s.t.p. will occupy 22.4 ℓ
   2.2 g of carbon dioxide at s.t.p. will occupy:

   $$22.4 \times \frac{2.2}{44} \ell$$

   $= 1.12 \ \ell \ (dm^3)$

3. 300 cm^3 of a gas at r.t.p. weighs 0.8 g. Find the relative molecular mass of the gas.

   300 cm^3 of the gas at r.t.p. weighs 0.8 g
   24 000 cm^3 of the gas at r.t.p. will weigh:

   $$0.8 \times \frac{24\,000}{300} \ g$$

   (Molar volume 24 ℓ)
   $= 64.0$ g

The relative molecular mass is therefore 64 g.
   To find the relative molecular mass is to find the mass of the molar volume at the temperature and pressure given. If the volume is at s.t.p., then the molar volume used is 22.4 ℓ (dm^3).
For example:
700 cm^3 of a gas at s.t.p. weighs 2 g. Find R.M.M.

700 cm^3 of the gas at s.t.p. weighs 2 g
22 400 cm^3 (22.4 ℓ) of the gas at s.t.p. will weigh:

$$2 \times \frac{22\,400}{700}$$

$= 64.0$ g

The relative molecular mass is therefore 64 g.

Questions

1. 100 cm^3 of hydrogen at s.t.p. contains x molecules. The number of molecules in the same volume of oxygen at s.t.p. is:
   A x
   B $2x$
   C $\frac{x}{2}$
   D $16x$

2. The Avogadro constant is:
   A the number of electrons needed to liberate one mole of copper from a copper(II) sulphate solution
   B the number of molecules in 1 g of hydrogen
   C the number of atoms in 12 g of carbon-12
   D the number of molecules in 16 g of oxygen.

3. The volume occupied by 16 g of oxygen at s.t.p. is:
   A 24 dm^3
   B 22.4 dm^3
   C 12 dm^3
   D 11.2 dm^3

4. The number of molecules in 0.001 g of hydrogen is:
   A 6.02×10^{20}
   B $\frac{6.02}{2} \times 10^{20}$
   C $\frac{6.02}{2} \times 10^{23}$
   D 6.02×10^{23}

5. 120 cm^3 of a gas at room temperature weighs 0.32 g. The relative molecular mass of the gas is:
   A 32 g   B 16 g   C 64 g   D 128 g

6. One volume of a gas X, combines with the same volume of another gas, Y, both gases being at the same temperature and pressure. Which of the following conclusions can be made concerning the volume of gaseous product at the same temperature and pressure as the reactants?
   A There will be two volumes of gaseous product.
   B One volume of gaseous product will be formed.
   C The volume of gaseous product cannot be predicted unless the chemical formulae of the reactants are known.
   D The volume of gaseous product can only be predicted if the experimentally determined equation is known.

7. Calculate the mass of one mole of molecules for the following substances:
   a hydrogen (H_2)
   b oxygen (O_2)
   c hydrogen chloride (HCl)
   d hydrogen sulphide (H_2S)
   e neon (Ne)
   f sulphur dioxide (SO_2).

8. Calculate the number of moles of molecules present in the following masses:
   a 10 g of argon
   b 1 g of hydrogen
   c 64 g of oxygen
   d 64 g of sulphur dioxide
   e 8.5 g of hydrogen sulphide
   f 18.25 g hydrogen chloride.

12 Chemical formulae and equations

Chemical formulae
The chemical formulae of compounds can be found by finding out the masses of the elements in a given mass of compound.

To determine the chemical formula of copper(II) oxide
Dry hydrogen gas can be passed over heated black copper(II) oxide until the mass of the copper remaining at the end of the reaction is constant. At this point, all the copper(II) oxide has been reduced to copper, according to the equation:

$$CuO(s) + H_2(g) \rightarrow Cu(s) + H_2O(g)$$

The following is a possible set of results from such an experiment.
- Mass of copper(II) oxide = 15.90 g
- Mass of copper remaining = 12.70 g
- Mass of oxygen removed = 3.20 g

So, 12.70 g of copper combines with 3.20 g of oxygen.

$\frac{12.70}{63.5}$ mole of copper atoms combines with

$\frac{3.20}{16}$ mole of oxygen.

This means that 0.2 mole of copper atoms combines with 0.2 mole of oxygen atoms.

One mole of copper atoms combines with one mole of oxygen atoms, i.e. one copper atom will combine with one oxygen atom.

The chemical formula of copper(II) oxide is therefore CuO.

This method can be used to find the chemical formulae of other compounds. Other methods are also available. For example, the amount of chloride in a mass of sodium chloride can be found by titrating with standard silver nitrate solution.

Empirical formula or simplest formula
The empirical formula of a compound is a formula giving the simplest ratio of the numbers of atoms of each element in the compound. It is usually calculated from the percentage of each element in the compound or from the mass of each element in a given mass of the compound. For example:

A hydrocarbon contains 85.7% of carbon. Find its empirical formula.

Since 85.7% is carbon combined with 14.3% of hydrogen, there will be 85.7 g of carbon and 14.3 g of hydrogen in 100 g of this hydrocarbon.

So, 85.7 g of carbon combines with 14.3 g of hydrogen.

$\frac{85.7}{12}$ moles of carbon atoms combines with

$\frac{14.3}{1}$ moles of hydrogen atoms.

This means that 7.14 moles of carbon atoms combine with 14.3 moles of hydrogen atoms.

One mole of carbon atoms combines with two moles of hydrogen atoms.

One atom of carbon combines with two atoms of hydrogen.

The simplest formula of the hydrocarbon is therefore CH_2.

If the relative molecular mass of the compound is 56 g, the molecular formula can be calculated as follows:

$$(CH_2)_n = 56$$
$$n(12 + 2) = 56$$
$$14n = 56$$
$$n = 4$$

The molecular formula is therefore C_4H_8.

The **molecular formula** gives the actual number of atoms of each element in a molecule of the compound.

Chemical equations
Chemical investigations can be carried out to obtain information that can lead to the writing of chemical equations. During a chemical reaction matter is neither gained nor lost. This principle must be observed when writing chemical equations. There must be the same number of atoms of each element on both sides of the equation.

Investigating the reaction between sodium hydroxide solution and dilute hydrochloric acid
A known concentration of hydrochloric acid is titrated against a known concentration of hydroxide. Methyl orange can be used as the indicator.

Result Concentration of hydrochloric acid in mol dm^{-3} = 0.1
Concentration of sodium hydroxide in mol dm^{-3} = 0.1
Volume of sodium hydroxide used in cm^3 = 25
Volume of hydrochloric acid used in cm^3 = 25

25 cm^3 of 0.1 mol dm^{-3} HCl neutralised 25 cm^3 of 0.1 mol dm^{-3} NaOH.

0.0025 mole of HCl neutralised 0.0025 mole of NaOH.

One mole of HCl will neutralise one mole of NaOH. Therefore part of the equation will be as follows:
$HCl(aq) + NaOH(aq) \rightarrow$

The equation can be completed if it can be ascertained what the products are. In this case, they are sodium chloride and water. The equation can be completed by writing in the formulae of the products and balancing the equation.
$HCl(aq) + NaOH(aq) \rightarrow NaCl(aq) + H_2O(l)$

Investigating the reaction between calcium carbonate and dilute hydrochloric acid

A known mass of calcium carbonate is reacted with dilute hydrochloric acid and the carbon dioxide evolved is collected in a gas syringe. The hydrochloric acid is first saturated with carbon dioxide by adding a little calcium carbonate before the syringe is connected. The apparatus used is shown in the diagram below.

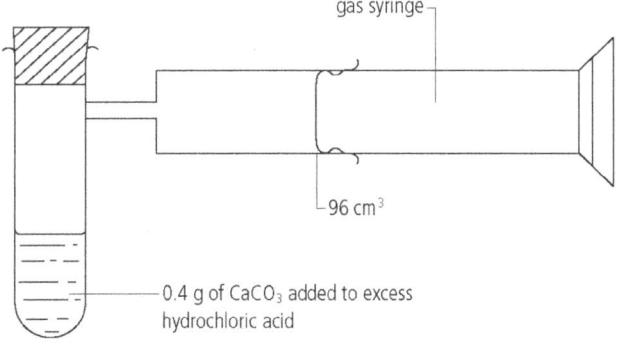

Mass of CaCO$_3$ used = 0.4 g
= $\frac{0.4}{100}$ mole
= 0.004 mole

Volume of CO$_2$ produced = 96 cm^3
= $\frac{96}{24\,000}$ mole

(Molar volume at room temperature and pressure is 24 000 cm^3)
= 0.004 mole

0.004 mole of calcium carbonate produced 0.004 mole of carbon dioxide.

One mole of calcium carbonate produced one mole of carbon dioxide.

Part of the equation can be written as:
$CaCO_3(s) + xHCl(aq) \rightarrow CO_2(g)$

Another experiment can be carried out to find the number of moles of HCl used. This can be done by starting with a standard HCl solution and titrating with standard NaOH to find the number of moles remaining after the reaction. The other products are calcium chloride and water.

The balanced equation is:
$CaCO_3(s) + 2HCl(aq) \rightarrow CaCl_2(aq) + H_2O(l) + CO_2(g)$

Investigating the reaction between barium chloride and dilute sulphuric acid by measuring the height of precipitate produced

1 cm^3 of 1 M sulphuric acid can be added to 5 cm^3 of 1 M barium chloride in a test tube. This can be repeated several times, each time increasing the volume of sulphuric acid by 1 cm^3. Each mixture is then centrifuged for the same amount of time and the heights of the precipitate measured. The test tubes used must be of the same dimensions.

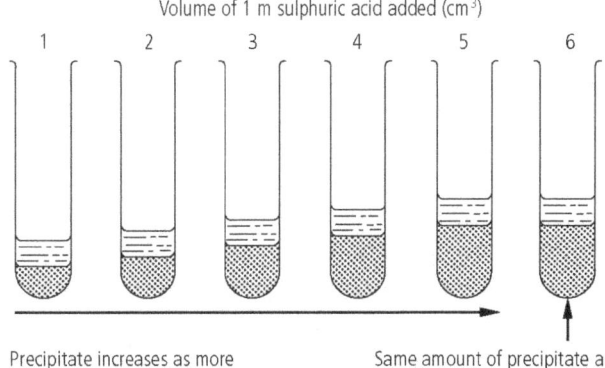

From the above results we can say that:
5 cm^3 of 1 M sulphuric acid reacts exactly with 5 cm^3 of 1 M barium chloride.

0.005 mole of H$_2$SO$_4$ reacts exactly with 0.005 mole of BaCl$_2$.

One mole of sulphuric acid reacts exactly with one mole of barium chloride.

The balanced equation will therefore be:
$BaCl_2(aq) + H_2SO_4(aq) \rightarrow BaSO_4(s) + 2HCl(aq)$

Alternatively, the mass of barium sulphate produced by using a fixed volume of molar barium chloride can be found and the equation completed by the balancing principle.

Balancing equations

Chemical equations can only be balanced by increasing the number of moles of the substance containing the element where the number of atoms needs increasing. For example, magnesium reacts with oxygen to form magnesium oxide. This reaction can be represented by the following equation:

$$Mg(s) + O_2(g) \rightarrow MgO(s)$$

This equation is unbalanced because there are two atoms of oxygen on the left-hand side and only one atom on the right-hand side. The number of moles of magnesium oxide can therefore be increased to two:

$$Mg(s) + O_2(g) \rightarrow 2MgO(s)$$

This necessitates an increase in the number of moles of magnesium to two. The balanced equation is thus:

$$2Mg(s) + O_2(g) \rightarrow 2MgO(s)$$

Some students are tempted to do the following:

$$Mg(s) + O_2(g) \rightarrow \cancel{MgO_2}(s)$$

This is wrong because the experimentally determined chemical formula of magnesium oxide is MgO **not** MgO_2. Never change the formula of a compound to balance a chemical equation.

Ionic equations

Very often, ionic equations are written to represent reactions in which ions are involved. The ionic equation tells exactly which ionic species are directly involved in the reaction. The other ions are usually referred to as spectator ions. Here are two examples.

Reaction between zinc and dilute sulphuric acid

The complete equation is:

$$Zn(s) + H_2SO_4(aq) \rightarrow ZnSO_4(aq) + H_2(g)$$

Expressing the ionic compounds as ions, you get:

$$Zn(s) + 2H^+(aq) + SO_4^{2-}(aq) \rightarrow Zn^{2+}(aq) + SO_4^{2-}(aq) + H_2(g)$$

As can be seen, sulphate ions are not involved in the reaction. They are spectator ions. The ionic equation is therefore:

$$Zn(s) + 2H^+(aq) \rightarrow Zn^{2+}(aq) + H_2(g)$$

Reaction between aqueous barium chloride and dilute sulphuric acid

The complete equation is:

$$BaCl_2(aq) + H_2SO_4(aq) \rightarrow BaSO_4(s) + 2HCl(aq)$$

Expressing the ionic compounds as ions you get:

$$Ba^{2+}(aq) + 2Cl^-(aq) + 2H^+(aq) + SO_4^{2-}(aq) \rightarrow BaSO_4(s) + 2H^+(aq) + 2Cl^-(aq)$$

The ionic equation is therefore:

$$Ba^{2+}(aq) + SO_4^{2-}(aq) \rightarrow BaSO_4(s)$$

Calculations involving equations

1. What mass of copper can be obtained if 13.0 g of zinc is added to excess copper(II) sulphate solution?
   The balanced equation is:
   $$CuSO_4(aq) + Zn(s) \rightarrow ZnSO_4(aq) + Cu(s)$$
   From equation:
   One mole of zinc will produce one mole of copper, i.e. 65 g of zinc will produce 63.5 g of copper
   13 g of zinc will produce:

   $$63.5 \times \frac{13}{65} \text{ g of copper}$$

   = 12.7 g of copper

2. What mass of magnesium oxide can be obtained by burning 1.2 g of magnesium in oxygen?
   The balanced equation is:
   $$2Mg(s) + O_2(g) \rightarrow 2MgO(s)$$
   From equation:
   2 moles of magnesium will produce 2 moles of magnesium oxide, i.e.
   48 g of magnesium will produce 80 g of magnesium oxide
   1.2 g of magnesium will produce:

   $$80 \times \frac{1.2}{48} \text{ g of magnesium oxide}$$

   = 2.0 g of magnesium oxide

3. What mass of copper is needed to produce 23.85 g of copper(II) oxide?
   The balanced equation is:
   $$2Cu(s) + O_2(g) \rightarrow 2CuO(s)$$
   From equation:
   2 moles of copper will be produced from 2 moles of copper(II) oxide, i.e.
   127 g of copper will be produced from 159 g of copper(II) oxide

   $$127 \times \frac{23.85}{159} \text{ g of copper will be produced from 23.85 g of copper(II) oxide}$$

   = 19.1 g of copper

Questions

1. In an experiment, 4.0 g of magnesium was burnt in oxygen to give 6.67 g of magnesium oxide. From this experiment it can be deduced that:
   - **A** 4 moles of magnesium will combine with 6.67 moles of oxygen
   - **B** 4 moles of magnesium will combine with 2.27 moles of oxygen
   - **C** 0.167 mole of magnesium will combine with 0.167 mole of oxygen atoms
   - **D** 0.167 mole of magnesium will combine with 0.417 mole of oxygen atoms.

2. 2.39 g of an oxide of lead was reduced to give 2.07 g of lead. The simplest formula of the oxide is:
   - **A** PbO
   - **B** PbO_2
   - **C** Pb_2O
   - **D** Pb_3O_4

3. A hydrocarbon contains 81.8% of carbon. The simplest formula of the hydrocarbon is:
   - **A** CH_2
   - **B** C_2H_4
   - **C** C_3H_6
   - **D** C_3H_8

4. If the relative molecular mass of the hydrocarbon is 44 g, what is the molecular formula?
   - **A** CH_2 **B** C_2H_4 **C** C_3H_6 **D** C_3H_8

5. The chemical formula of carbon dioxide is CO_2. The percentage of carbon in one mole of carbon dioxide is approximately:
   - **A** 12 **B** 27 **C** 32 **D** 43

6. Which of the methods below can provide the evidence needed to write the chemical equation of a reaction?
   - I Complete reduction of an oxide.
   - II Neutralisation reaction between acid and alkali solutions of known concentrations.
   - III Measuring the heights of precipitates formed between two solutions of known concentration.
   - **A** I, II and III
   - **B** I and II only
   - **C** II and III only
   - **D** III only

7. Which of the following can be deduced from the molecular formula of a compound?
   - I The ratio of the number of atoms of each element in the compound.
   - II The number of atoms of each element in the compound.
   - III The relative molecular mass of the compound.
   - **A** I, II and III
   - **B** I and II only
   - **C** II and III only
   - **D** I only

8. For which of the following reactions between pairs of substances can equations be written by measuring the heights of precipitate obtained?
   - I barium nitrate and sodium sulphate
   - II lead nitrate and potassium iodine
   - III barium nitrate and sodium chloride
   - **A** I, II and III
   - **B** I and II only
   - **C** II and III only
   - **D** I only

9. In a balanced chemical equation there are an equal number of:
   - **A** molecules of substances on both sides of the equation
   - **B** moles of substances on both sides of the equation
   - **C** atoms of each element on both sides of the equation
   - **D** ions on both sides of the equation.

10. Which of the following represents the ionic equation for the reaction between zinc metal and copper(II) sulphate solution?
    - **A** $Zn(s) + Cu^{2+}(aq) + SO_4^{2-}(aq) \rightarrow Zn^{2+}(aq) + SO_4^{2-}(aq) + Cu(s)$
    - **B** $Zn(s) + Cu^{2+}(aq) \rightarrow Zn^{2+}(aq) + Cu(s)$
    - **C** $Zn^{2+}(s) + Cu^{2+}(aq) \rightarrow Zn^{2+}(aq) + Cu(s)$
    - **D** $Zn(s) + Cu^{2+}(aq) \rightarrow Zn^{2+}(aq) + Cu^{2+}(s)$

11. 4.78 g of an oxide of a metal (M = 207) was reduced to give 4.14 g of the metal.
    - a i What mass of oxygen combined with 4.14 g of the metal?
        ii How many moles of oxygen atoms are there in this mass?
    - b How many moles of the metal atoms are there in 4.14 g of it?
    - c How many moles of oxygen atoms will combine with one mole of the metal M?
    - d What is the formula of the oxide?

12. 5.85 g of sodium chloride is dissolved in a volumetric flask to make 1 dm^3 of solution. 10 cm^3 of this solution requires 10 cm^3 of 0.1 mol dm^{-3} silver nitrate solution for complete reaction. The chemical formula of silver chloride is AgCl.
    - a How many moles of silver nitrate are contained in 10 cm^3 of 0.1 mole dm^{-3} solution of it?
    - b How many moles of chloride ions will this solution react with?
    - c i How many moles of chloride ions are contained in 1 dm^3 of solution?
        ii What mass of chloride is this?
    - d i How many grams of sodium are there in the 5.85 g of the solution?
        ii How many moles of sodium ions is this?
    - e How many moles of sodium ions will combine with one mole of chloride ions?
    - f What is the formula for sodium chloride?

13 Volumetric analysis

Standard solutions

A standard solution is one of known concentration. The standard used in chemistry today is mol dm^{-3} concentration.

A 1 M solution is one that contains 1 mole of a substance in 1 cubic decimetre (1 litre) of solution, for example a 1 M solution of sulphuric acid (R.M.M. = 98) will contain 98 g of sulphuric acid in 1 dm^3 (1 litre) of solution.

If a solution contains 0.1 mole of a substance in 1 dm^3 of solution, it is usually written as 0.1 M. The M means mol dm^{-3}. For example 0.2 M NaOH means there is 0.2 mole of sodium hydroxide in 1 dm^3 of solution. Here are some examples.

1. What mass of sodium hydroxide is needed to make 250 cm^3 of 0.1 M sodium hydroxide solution?

   1 000 cm^3 of the solution must contain 0.1 mole of NaOH.

   250 cm^3 of the solution must contain:
   $$\frac{0.1 \times 250}{1\,000} \text{ mole}$$
   $$= 0.0250 \text{ mole}$$
   1 mole of sodium hydroxide = 40 g
   Mass of NaOH needed = 0.025 × 40
   = 1.0 g

2. 50.0 cm^3 of a solution contains 0.490 g of sulphuric acid. What is the concentration of this solution in mol dm^{-3}? (R.M.M. of H_2SO_4 = 98)

   50.0 cm^3 of sulphuric acid solution contains 0.490 g.
   1 000 cm^3 of sulphuric acid solution will contain:
   $$0.49 \times \frac{1\,000}{50}$$
   = 9.80 g
   1 mole of H_2SO_4 = 98 g
   Number of moles in 9.8 g $\frac{9.8}{98}$
   = 0.1 mol dm^{-3}
   = 0.1 M

Remember: find the number of moles in 1 dm^3 (1 000 cm^3) of solution.

Preparation of standard solution

There are a few substances that can be weighed directly to make a solution of exact concentration. These substances are referred to as primary standards, for example, anhydrous sodium carbonate and ethanedioic acid (oxalic acid). For most other substances, only solutions of approximate concentrations can be made by weighing, and then their exact concentrations are found by titration.

Preparation of 0.1 M Na_2CO_3 solution

1. The mass of Na_2CO_3 required is 2.65 g. This mass can be obtained by heating anhydrous sodium carbonate for about 15 minutes and then allowing it to dry in a desiccator. (If it is left to cool in the air it will absorb moisture from the atmosphere on cooling.) The required mass of sodium carbonate is then weighed using a clean, dry watch glass or weighing bottle. The balance used must be able to weigh to an accuracy of at least two decimal places.

2. The sodium carbonate is then transferred to a beaker containing 60 cm^3 of hot distilled water. Ensure that *all* the solid is transferred to the beaker by washing the watch glass/weighing bottle with distilled water from a wash bottle. The mixture is stirred to dissolve the solid.

3. After being allowed to cool, a funnel is used to carefully transfer the solution to a volumetric flask. The beaker and funnel must be rinsed a couple of times with distilled water to ensure that all the sodium carbonate solution is transferred to the flask. Distilled water is then carefully added to bring the solution up to the 250 cm^3 mark. The meniscus must be observed at eye level. The solution can then be thoroughly shaken to ensure uniform mixing. After shaking, the meniscus might be below the 250 cm^3 mark. The solution must *not* be topped up to the 250 cm^3 at this stage as there is already that volume of the solution in the flask – some of the solution is now on the stopper and the upper neck of the flask.

Preparation of an approximately 0.1 M H_2SO_4 solution

Solutions of exact concentrations of sulphuric acid cannot be made up directly because concentrated sulphuric acid absorbs moisture from the atmosphere. Solutions of approximate concentrations of such substances are usually made up and their exact concentrations are then found by titration. Since concentrated sulphuric acid is liquid, the mass needed is obtained using the mass–volume–density relationship. The mass of sulphuric acid required to make 250 cm^3 of solution is 2.45 g. The density of concentrated sulphuric acid is approximately 1.80 g dm^{-3}. The volume containing 2.45 g is therefore 2.45 ÷ 1.8 = 1.3 cm^3.

1. Some distilled water is placed into a 250 cm^3 volumetric flask and 1.3 cm^3 of concentrated sulphuric acid is run into it from a burette. The mixture is then swirled and carefully made up to the 250 cm^3 mark when cooled. The solution is approximately 0.1 M.

Titration

The exact concentration of the approximately 0.1 M sulphuric acid can be obtained using the 0.1 M Na_2CO_3 solution. The method normally used is titration.

1. The sulphuric acid is placed in a clean burette that has been rinsed with some of the sulphuric acid, which was then discarded. The burette is an instrument used to deliver accurately varying volumes of solutions. The most common one in use is of 50 cm^3 capacity. It is graduated to 0.1 cm^3. It can therefore be read to 0.05 cm^3 accuracy. All burette readings must therefore be done to two decimal place accuracy. When using the burette, make sure that (a) there is a continuous column of solution from the tip of the burette to the 0 cm^3 mark and (b) there are no bubbles on the walls of the burette. If air bubbles appear, the burette must be emptied, properly washed with soap and, after rinsing with distilled water and the solution to be used in it, filled again.

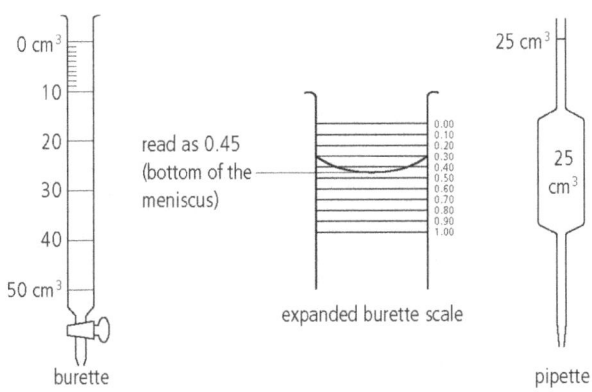

2. 25.0 cm^3 of sodium carbonate is transferred to a titration flask (conical flask) using a pipette. A pipette is an instrument used to measure an accurate volume of solution (usually 25 cm^3). Like the burette, the pipette must be read at eye level. The pipette should also be properly washed and then rinsed with some of the solution it is to measure. The pipette is usually filled with solution by sucking with the mouth (if pipette filters or bulbs are not available). The tip of the pipette must be placed well into the solution to avoid sucking air into the pipette which will cause some of the solution to get into the mouth. If this happens, quickly spit out the solution and wash out your mouth. The solution is normally sucked up above the graduation mark and the fore-finger placed on the mouth of the pipette. The solution is then slowly let out into the conical flask. The tip of the pipette is then allowed to touch the surface of the solution in the flask and then withdrawn. NEVER BLOW OUT THE DROP OF SOLUTION REMAINING IN THE PIPETTE. A pipette is made to operate in this way.

3. The next step is to find out what volume of sulphuric acid will exactly neutralise the 25 cm^3 of sodium carbonate solution. An indicator is used to do this. Some indicators commonly used are:

Indicator	Alkaline	Acidic	Neutral
Methyl orange	Yellow	Red	Orange
Screened methyl orange	Green	Violet	Green
Phenolphthalein	Pink	Colourless	Colourless

Phenolphthalein is suitable for titration involving weak acids, whereas methyl orange is suitable for titration involving strong acids.

The one used for this titration is methyl orange. A few drops of the indicator are added to the sodium carbonate solution, giving it a yellow colour. Sulphuric acid is then added from the burette, about 1 cm^3 at a time, swirling the flask continuously. The acid is added until there is a permanent colour change. This first (rough) titration gives the approximate volume of sulphuric acid needed to neutralise the carbonate solution. The titration is repeated taking care to add the solution drop by drop from about 1 cm^3 less than the first titration. One drop of the acid solution will change the colour of the carbonate solution from yellow to orange. This is the **end-point** of the titration. The titration must be repeated until two results are within 0.10 cm^3 of each other. The mean of the two accurate titrations is the volume of sulphuric acid needed to neutralise the sodium carbonate. The concentration of the sulphuric acid can now be calculated (see next chapter). Here are some sample results.

Titration number	Rough	Accurate 1	Accurate 2
End-point	26.60	26.50	26.60
Starting point	0.00	0.00	0.20
Volume of sulphuric acid used (cm^3)	26.50	26.50	26.40

The mean volume of sulphuric acid is therefore:
$$\frac{26.50 + 26.40}{2} = 26.45 \text{ cm}^3$$

26.45 cm³ of sulphuric acid reacted exactly with 25 cm³ of sodium carbonate.

Thermometric titrations

For some types of titrations, indicators cannot be used. For example, for a weak acid–weak alkali titration, no suitable indicator is available. The titration can be carried out thermometrically. The reaction between an acid and an alkali is exothermic (Chapter 20) so the temperature will increase until the reaction stops. The reaction can be carried out in much the same way as described before, except that the temperature of the mixture is taken after addition of fixed volumes of sulphuric acid. Some typical results are given below.

Volume of sulphuric acid added (cm³)	0	5	10	15	20	25	30	35
Temperature (°C)	25	28	31	34	37	40	38.8	36.7

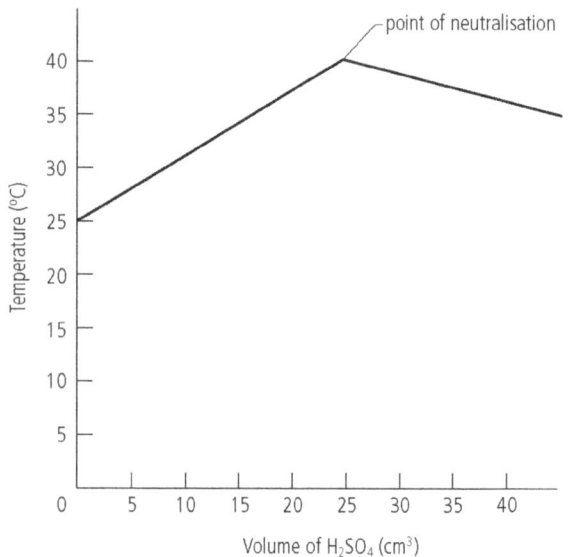

Questions

1. A standard solution is one:
   A of known concentration
   B that contains 1 mole of substance in 1 dm³ of solution
   C that neutralises a 1 M solution of sodium hydroxide
   D that contains a known mass of solute in any volume of solution.

2. A molar solution is one that contains:
   A 1 mole of a substance in 1 litre of water
   B 1 mole of substance in 1 000 g of water
   C 1 mole of substance in 1 litre of solution
   D 1 gram of substance in 1 litre of solution.

3. The number of moles of sulphuric acid (H_2SO_4) in 25 cm³ of a 0.1 mol dm⁻³ solution of it is:
   A 0.1   C 4
   B 0.25   D 0.0025

4. 25 cm³ of a solution of sodium hydroxide contains 0.4 g. The concentration of this solution in mole dm⁻³ is:
   A 4   C 0.04
   B 0.4   D 0.00025

5. A standard solution of sodium carbonate can be made by dissolving a known mass of:
   A sodium carbonate crystals in some water in a beaker and then making the solution up to the required volume
   B sodium carbonate crystals in some water in a volumetric flask and then making the solution up to the required volume
   C anhydrous sodium carbonate in a beaker and making the solution up to the required volume
   D anhydrous sodium carbonate in a beaker, transferring it to a volumetric flask, and then making the solution up to the required volume.

6. Which of the following substances can be directly measured out to prepare a standard solution?
   A anhydrous sodium carbonate
   B sodium hydroxide
   C sulphuric acid
   D sodium carbonate crystals

7. The colour at the end point of a titration between an acid and an alkali using methyl orange as the indicator, is:
   A yellow   C orange
   B red   D pink

8. In a titration, a 0.1 mol dm⁻³ sodium carbonate solution was used to find the concentration of a sulphuric acid solution.
   a i Which solution would you place in the burette?
      ii What precautions should be observed when using the burette?
   b Explain what precautions you should take to ensure accuracy when using the pipette.
   c Name an indicator that would be suitable for this reaction?
   d How would you know when the reaction is exactly completed?
   e How many times would you repeat the titration?
   f What would you regard as consistent results?
   g If 26.5 cm³ of sulphuric acid is needed to neutralise 25 cm³ of the sodium carbonate solution, what is the molar concentration of the acid solution?

14 Calculations involving volumetric analysis

The following are some typical calculations often encountered in volumetric analysis. All calculations must be done to three significant figures.

1. 26.4 cm³ of sulphuric acid neutralises 25.0 cm³ of 0.100 M Na_2CO_3. What is the concentration of the sulphuric acid solution in moles?
Two methods can be used to find the answer.

Method I

From first principles:
Equation:
$Na_2CO_3(aq) + H_2SO_4(aq) \rightarrow Na_2SO_4(aq) + H_2O(l) + CO_2(aq)$

25.0 cm³ of 0.1 M Na_2CO_3 contains $\dfrac{0.100 \times 25.0}{1\,000}$ mole
= 0.00250 mole

From equation:
1 mole Na_2CO_3 reacts exactly with 1 mole H_2SO_4
0.00250 mole Na_2CO_3 will react exactly with 0.00250 mole H_2SO_4
26.45 cm³ of H_2SO_4 must contain 0.00250 mole
Hence, 1 000 cm³ of H_2SO_4 contains:

$0.00250 \times \dfrac{1\,000}{26.45}$

= 0.0945 mole
= 0.0945 M

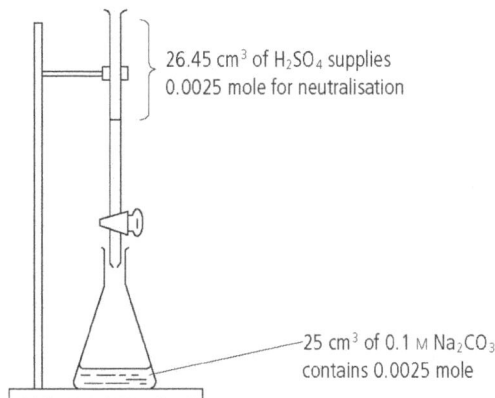

26.45 cm³ of H_2SO_4 supplies 0.0025 mole for neutralisation

25 cm³ of 0.1 M Na_2CO_3 contains 0.0025 mole

Method II

By formula: $\dfrac{M_A V_A}{M_B V_B} = \dfrac{a}{b}$

M_A = concentration of acid
V_A = volume of acid
M_B = concentration of base
V_B = volume of base
a = stoichiometric coefficient of acid
b = stoichiometric coefficient of base

The stoichiometric coefficient is the figure used in the balanced chemical equation. In this case both a and b are 1.

$\dfrac{M_A V_A}{M_B V_B} = \dfrac{1}{1}$

$M_A = \dfrac{M_B V_B}{V_A} = \dfrac{0.100 \times 25.0}{26.45} = 0.0945$ M

2. 25.0 cm³ of 0.100 M NaOH reacts exactly with 50.0 cm³ of 0.0500 M HA (an acid). Use the information given to write an equation for the reaction between the alkali and acid.
25.0 cm³ of 0.100 M NaOH contains:

$0.100 \times \dfrac{25.0}{1\,000}$ mole = 0.0025 mole

50.0 cm³ of 0.0500 M HA contains:

$0.0500 \times \dfrac{25.0}{1\,000}$ mole = 0.00250 mole

0.00250 mole of NaOH reacts exactly with 0.00250 mole HA
1 mole of NaOH reacts exactly with 1 mole of HA

Equation:
$NaOH(aq) + HA(aq) \rightarrow NaA(aq) + H_2O(aq)$

3. 25.0 cm³ of a solution of an acid containing 30.0 g dm⁻³ acid needed 16.3 cm³ of 1 M sodium hydroxide for neutralisation. If the molecular mass of the acid is 92.0 g, calculate its basicity.

Concentration of acid = $\dfrac{\text{Mass in g dm}^{-3}}{\text{Mass of 1 mole}}$

= $\dfrac{30.0}{92.0}$ = 0.326 M

25.0 cm³ of 0.326 M acid solution contains:

$\dfrac{0.326 \times 25.0}{1\,000}$ mole

= 0.008 12 mole

16.3 cm³ of 1 M sodium hydroxide contains

$\dfrac{1 \times 16.3}{1\,000}$ mole

= 0.0163 mole

0.00812 mole of acid reacts exactly with 0.0163 mole of NaOH

1 mole of acid reacts exactly with:

$$\frac{0.0163}{0.008\,12} \text{ mole of NaOH}$$

= 2 moles NaOH
Basicity of acid = 2

4. 26.5 cm³ of 0.100 M HCl react exactly with 25.0 cm³ of a carbonate solution (X_2CO_3) containing 12.2 g dm⁻³. Find the relative atomic mass of X and use the periodic table to identify the element.

Equation:
$2HCl(aq) + X_2CO_3(aq) \rightarrow XCl_2(aq) + H_2O(aq) + CO_2(g)$

26.5 cm³ of 0.1 M HCl contains:

$$0.100 \times \frac{26.5}{1\,000} \text{ mole}$$

= 0.002 65 mole

From equation:
0.002 65 mole of HCl will react with:

$$\frac{0.002\,65}{2} \text{ mole of the carbonate}$$

25.0 cm³ of carbonate solution contains 0.001 325 mole
1 000 cm³ of carbonate solution contains:

$$\frac{0.001\,325 \times 1000}{25.0} = 0.0530 \text{ mole dm}^{-3}$$

So, 0.0530 mole of carbonate (X_2CO_3) = 12.2 g

1 mole of $X_2CO_3 = \frac{12.2}{0.0530}$

= 230 g
X_2CO_3 = 230   C = 12, 3O = 48
                     CO_3 = 60
2X = 230 − 60
   = 170
X = 85
Therefore X is rubidium.

5. 12.0 g of a mixture of sodium chloride and anhydrous sodium carbonate were made up to 1 dm³ of aqueous solution. 25.0 cm³ of this solution required 20.0 cm³ of 0.200 M hydrochloric acid for neutralisation. What was the mass of sodium chloride in the mixture?

The hydrochloric acid was used to neutralise the carbonate in the solution.
$Na_2CO_3(aq) + 2HCl(aq) \rightarrow 2NaCl(aq) + H_2O(l) + CO_2(g)$

20.0 cm³ of 0.200 M HCl contains:

$$\frac{0.200 \times 20.0}{1\,000} \text{ mole} = 0.00400 \text{ mole}$$

0.00400 mole of HCl reacts exactly with 0.00200 mole of Na_2CO_3.
25.0 cm³ of the solution contains 0.00200 mole of CO_3^{2-}

1 000 cm³ of the solution contains $\frac{0.00200 \times 1\,000}{25.0}$ mole

= 0.0800 mole
= 0.0800 × 106 g
= 8.48 g
Mass of sodium chloride in mixture = 12.0 − 8.48
                                    = 3.52 g

Questions

1. 20.0 cm³ of 0.050 mol dm⁻³ sulphuric acid neutralised 25.0 cm³ of sodium hydroxide solution. What is the concentration in moles of the sodium hydroxide solution?

2. 25.0 cm³ of a 0.100 mole dm⁻³ sodium hydroxide solution required 30.0 cm³ of sulphuric acid for neutralisation. Calculate the concentration of sulphuric acid in (a) mole dm⁻³ (b) g dm⁻³.

3. 50.0 cm³ of hydrochloric acid were needed to neutralise 25 cm³ of 0.100 mole dm⁻³ potassium hydroxide. What was the concentration of the acid solution in moles?

4. 40.0 cm³ of hydrochloric acid were needed to neutralise 25.0 cm³ of 0.0500 mol dm⁻³ sodium carbonate solution. Calculate the concentration of hydrochloric acid in (a) mole dm⁻³ (b) g dm⁻³.

5. 30.0 cm³ of a solution of an acid containing 38.4 g dm⁻³ needed 25.0 cm³ of 0.500 mole dm⁻³ sodium carbonate for neutralisation. If the molecular mass of the acid is 92.0 g, calculate its basicity.

6. 35.0 cm³ of an acid solution containing 3.65 g dm⁻³ required 25.0 cm³ of 0.140 mole dm⁻³ sodium hydroxide solution for neutralisation. If the molecular mass of the acid is 36.5 g, calculate its basicity.

7. 30.0 cm³ of a hydrochloric acid solution containing 1.52 g dm⁻³ reacted exactly with 25.0 cm³ of a hydroxide solution (XOH) containing 7.50 g dm⁻³. Find the relative atomic mass of X and use the periodic table to identity the element.

15 Electrochemistry

Electrochemical cells

Consider the following arrangements:

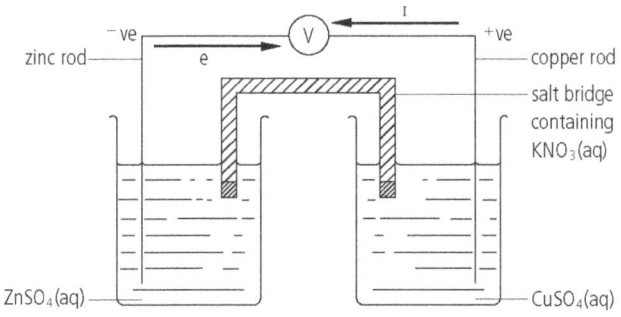

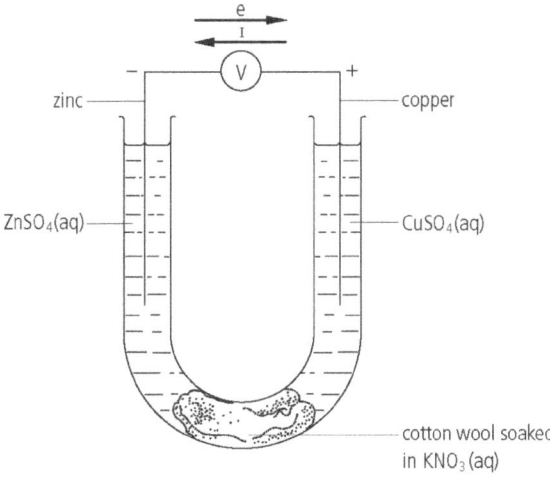

Both diagrams represent electrochemical cells. They are used to convert chemical energy into electrical energy. Consider the cells as comprising two half cells.

Zinc half cell	Copper half cell
Zinc dissolves from electrode and goes into solution as zinc ions (Zn^{2+}).	Copper ions (Cu^{2+}) from solution are discharged and deposited as copper on the copper electrode.
$Zn(s) \rightarrow Zn^{2+}(aq) + 2e$	$Cu^{2+}(aq) + 2e \rightarrow Cu(s)$

Zinc has a greater tendency to lose electrons than copper, i.e. zinc is more electropositive. Electrons from the zinc half cells flow across the external circuit to the copper half cell. This results in a flow of conventional current from copper to zinc. Copper is therefore the positive terminal of the cell.

Purpose of the salt bridge

The salt bridge is a device that allows ions to travel in and out of the half cells. It can be made by soaking any absorbent matter in an electrolyte (usually KNO_3). In some cells (Daniell cells) the salt bridge is a porcelain porous pot.

In the operation of the cell, electrons flow from the zinc half cell to the copper half cell. This causes a build-up of positive charges in the zinc half cell and of negative charges in the copper half cell. This situation will oppose the flow of electrons from zinc to copper, causing a cessation in the flow of current from copper to zinc. The salt bridge prevents this from happening. It allows positive ions to flow out of the zinc half cell into the salt bridge and negative ions from the salt bridge to flow into the zinc half cell. The opposite occurs at the other half cell. For reasons given below, the zinc half cell is called the **oxidation** half cell and the copper one is called the **reduction** half cell.

Oxidation and reduction (redox processes)

Oxidation and reduction are opposite processes which occur simultaneously.

Oxidation was first described as a gain in oxygen and reduction as a loss of oxygen, for example:
$CuO(s) + H_2(g) \rightarrow Cu(s) + H_2O(l)$
reduced   oxidised

In the above reaction, copper(II) oxide is reduced and hydrogen is oxidised. Hydrogen and oxygen were perceived as chemical opposites so the definition of the processes was extended to include hydrogen.

Oxidation is the loss of hydrogen and reduction the gain of hydrogen, for example:
$2H_2(g) + O_2(g) \rightarrow 2H_2O(l)$
oxidised reduced

Oxidation is now described as a loss of electrons and reduction as a gain of electrons. A useful mnemonic is OIL RIG (Oxidation is Loss, Reduction is Gain).
$Cu^{2+}(aq) + Zn(s) \rightarrow Zn^{2+}(aq) + Cu(s)$
reduced   oxidised

$Cu^{2+}(aq) + 2e \rightarrow Cu(s)$ (gain of electrons by Cu^{2+})
$Zn(s) \rightarrow Zn^{2+}(aq) + 2e$ (loss of electrons by Zn)
In all of these reactions, remember that the substances reacting are on the left-hand side of the equation, so the species that are oxidised or reduced will also be found on that side and not on the right-hand side.

Oxidation number concept

There are many reactions which do not involve transfer of electrons, but are redox processes, for example:

$$2H_2(g) + O_2(g) \rightarrow 2H_2O(l)$$

The concept of oxidation number (or state) was introduced to take care of these situations. Oxidation is an increase in oxidation number (state) and reduction is a decrease in oxidation number (state).

Rules for assigning oxidation numbers

1. All uncombined elements have an oxidation number of zero.
2. In an ionic compound involving a metal and non-metal, the oxidation number is in charge of the ions, for example, in Na^+Cl^-, sodium has an oxidation number of +1 and chlorine an oxidation number of –1.
3. The algebraic sum of the oxidation numbers in a compound is zero, for example in 2 above: Na = +1, Cl = –1, (+1) + (–1) = 0.
4. In compounds, oxygen always has an oxidation number of –2, except in peroxides when it has an oxidation number of –1.
5. In compounds, hydrogen always has an oxidation number of +1, but in metallic hydrides it is –1.
6. In complex anions, the charge on the anion is the algebraic sum of the oxidation numbers of the elements in the anion. The more electropositive element usually has the positive oxidation number and the other the negative, for example MnO_4^-:
   4 O has a total oxidation number of –8
   The net charge on the ion is –1
   Oxidation number of Mn + (–8) = –1
   Oxidation number of Mn = +7

SO_4^{2-} : S + (–8)	= –2
S	= +6
Oxidation number of S	= +6
$Cr_2O_7^{2-}$: 2Cr + 7(–2)	= –2
2Cr + (–14)	= –2
2Cr	= 12
Cr	= +6
Oxidation number of Cr	= +6

Questions

1. a Choose two metals that can be used to set up an electrochemical cell.
   b Draw a labelled diagram of the cell.
   c Write equations to show the reactions taking place in (i) the oxidation half cell and (ii) the reduction half cell.
   d Indicate on your diagram (i) the direction of flow of electric current (ii) the positive terminal and (iii) the negative terminal.
   e State which ions are (i) entering and (ii) leaving the salt bridge in each half cell.

2. Which species is (a) oxidised and (b) reduced (c) the oxidising agent and (d) the reducing agent in the following reactions?
   i $Zn(s) + 2H^+(aq) \rightarrow Zn^{2+}(aq) + H_2(aq)$
   ii $Cl_2(aq) + I^-(aq) \rightarrow I_2(aq) + 2Cl^-(aq)$
   iii $2H_2O_2(l) \rightarrow 1H_2O(l) + O_2(g)$
   iv $2FeCl_2(aq) + Cl_2(aq) \rightarrow 2FeCl_3(aq)$
   v $Cu^{2+}(aq) + Mg(s) \rightarrow Cu(s) + Mg^{2+}(aq)$
   vi $2Mg(s) + O_2(g) \rightarrow 2MgO(s)$
   vii $Fe_2O_3(s) + 3CO(g) \rightarrow 2Fe(s) + 3CO_2(g)$
   vii $2Na(s) + Cl_2(g) \rightarrow 2NaCl(s)$
   ix $H_2(g) + Cl_2(g) \rightarrow 2HCl(g)$

3. What is the oxidation number of the first element in the following molecules or ions:
   a MnO_2 d NH_3 g V_2O_5 j B_2O_3
   b MnO_4^{2-} e CO_3^{2-} h CrO_4
   c SO_3^{2-} f Na_2O_2 i $MgCl_2$

4. The anode of an electrolytic cell:
   A reduces anions
   B acts as a reducing agent
   C acts as an oxidising agents
   D supplies electrons.

5. Oxidation is said to have taken place when there is:
   A a gain of electrons
   B a loss of electrons
   C a decrease in oxidation number
   D a decrease in oxygen content.

6. The oxidation number of nitrogen in NO_3^- is:
   A +2 B –5 C +4 D +5

7. Consider the equation $H^+(aq) + OH^-(aq) \rightarrow H_2O$. Which of the following is true?
   A Hydrogen ions are reduced.
   B Hydrogen ions are oxidised.
   C Hydroxide ions are oxidised.
   D None of the ions are oxidised or reduced.

8. X and Y are two metals. Element X is more electropositive than Y. If the two metals are used in an electrochemical cell, what will occur?
   A There will be a flow of electricity from X to Y.
   B There will be a flow of electrons from X to Y.
   C There will be a flow of electrons from Y to X.
   D X will be the positive terminal of the cell.

9. Consider the ion ZO_3^{x-}. If the oxidation number of Z is +4, x will be:
   A 1 B 2 C 3 D 4

10. Which of these pairs of metals are most suitable to use as electrodes in an electrochemical cell?
    A K and Na C Mg and Pb
    B K and Cu D Pb and Cu

16 Electrochemical and reactivity series

An electrochemical cell can be formed between a metal/metal ion system and a hydrogen electrode as shown in the diagram below.

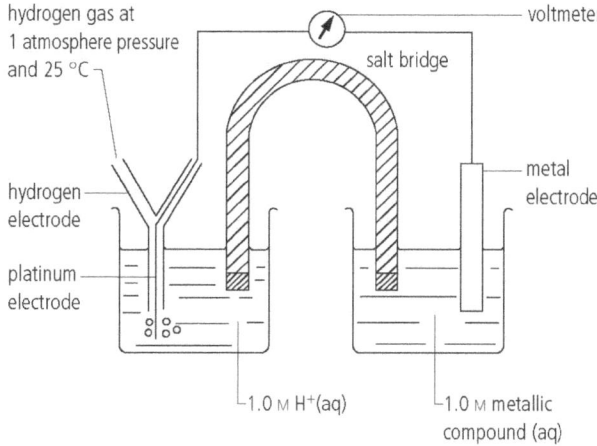

The potential recorded is referred to as the electrode potential of the metal. This is the maximum voltage of the cell, i.e. the cell e.m.f. The hydrogen electrode is chosen as a standard reference electrode and assigned a potential of 0.00 V. Therefore, the electrode potential of all metal/metal ion systems can be compared with the hydrogen electrode. Under the following conditions, the electrode potential recorded is called the standard electrode potential (S.E.P.).
- Concentration of solutions: 1 mol dm^{-3}
- Hydrogen gas: 1 atmosphere pressure
- Temperature: 25 °C

Metals that are more electropositive than hydrogen are given a negative standard electrode potential and those that are less electropositive are given a positive standard electrode potential. Some values are listed below.

Element	S.E.P.(V)
K	−2.92
Ca	−2.87
Na	−2.71
Mg	−2.37
Al	−2.00
Zn	−1.10
Fe	−0.78
Pb	−0.47
H	+0.00
Cu	+0.34
Ag	+0.80

Metals with a negative S.E.P. make up the oxidation half cell M(s) → M^{2+}(aq) + 2e. When the metals are arranged in the order they appear in the table, the series is called the **electrochemical series** (E.C.S.).

Reactivity series

The reactivity series is formed on the basis of the chemical reactivity of the metals, with the most reactive being placed first and the least reactive last. The reactivity can be based on the following:
a Displacement reaction. Zinc displaces copper metal from aqueous copper(II) solutions. Therefore zinc is more reactive than copper.
b Reactions with oxygen.
c Reduction of oxides by hydrogen and/or carbon.
d Relative ease of decomposition of their compounds, for example, nitrates, carbonates, hydroxides.

The major difference in the order of metals between the electrochemical series (E.C.S.) and the reactivity series is that in the E.C.S., calcium comes before sodium, but in the reactivity series calcium comes after sodium.

E.C.S.	K Ca Na Mg Al Zn Fe Pb H Cu Ag Au
Reactivity series	K Na Ca Mg Al Zn Fe Pb H Cu Ag Au

The electrochemical series and the reactivity series can be used in many ways.
a Metals that are higher in the E.C.S. can displace metals that are lower in the E.C.S. from an aqueous solution of their ions, for example:
$$Mg(s) + Cu^{2+}(aq) \rightarrow Mg^{2+}(aq) + Cu(s)$$
b Metals above hydrogen in the E.C.S. can displace hydrogen from dilute acids. Lead reacts very slowly with acids, for example:
$$Zn(s) + 2H^+(aq) \rightarrow Zn^{2+}(aq) + H_2(g)$$
c The series can be used as a guide to the general reactivity of the metals. The most reactive metals will be at the top of the series.

On the following page we demonstrate the change in reactivity as the series is descended.

Reaction of metals with water

K reacts violently with cold water to give a strongly alkaline solution and liberates hydrogen gas.

Na reacts the same as potassium but less violently.

Ca has a vigorous reaction with cold water giving an alkaline solution and liberating hydrogen gas.

Mg has a very slow reaction giving a slightly alkaline solution and liberating hydrogen gas.

Reaction of metals with steam

Mg, Al, Zn and Fe react with steam to give the metallic oxide and liberate hydrogen gas, for example:

$Zn(s) + H_2O(g) \rightarrow ZnO(s) + H_2(g)$

Metals lower than hydrogen will not react with water or steam.

Reaction with oxygen

K, Na and Ca will combine readily with oxygen from the air to form their oxides.

Mg to Fe will burn readily in air to form their oxides.

Pb and Cu will form oxides when heated in the air.

Reduction of oxides by hydrogen

The oxides of elements from Fe downwards are reduced to metal by hydrogen gas, for example:

$CuO(s) + H_2(g) \rightarrow H_2O(l) + Cu(s)$

The following properties demonstrate the trend in stability and solubility of the metal compounds as the series is descended.

Action of heat on hydroxides

KOH and NaOH are not decomposed at the temperature of the Bunsen flame.

All the other hydroxides are decomposed to give their oxides and water, for example:

$Mg(OH)_2(s) \rightarrow MgO(s) + H_2O(l)$

Action of heat on carbonates

K_2CO_3 and Na_2CO_3 are not decomposed at the temperature of the Bunsen flame.

All the other carbonates are decomposed to give their oxide and carbon dioxide, for example:

$CaCO_3(s) \rightarrow CaO(s) + CO_2(g)$

Action of heat on nitrates

The nitrates of sodium and potassium decompose to give their nitrites and oxygen, for example:

$NaNO_3(s) \rightarrow NaNO_2(s) + O_2(g)$

The nitrates of the metals from calcium to copper decompose to give their respective oxides, nitrogen dioxide (a brown gas) and oxygen, for example:

$2Pb(NO_3)_2(s) \rightarrow 2PbO(s) + 4NO_2(g) + O_2(g)$

Nitrates below copper, for example, silver nitrate, decompose to give the metal, nitrogen dioxide and oxygen:

$2AgNO_3(s) \rightarrow 2Ag(s) + 2NO_2(g) + O_2(g)$

Solubility of hydroxides and carbonates

The hydroxides and carbonates of sodium and potassium are all soluble in water. Calcium hydroxide is only slightly soluble in water. All the other metallic hydroxides and carbonates are insoluble in water.

Questions

1. Magnesium is above copper in the electrochemical series. What will be observed after a long time if excess magnesium is added to aqueous copper(II) sulphate?
   A grey pieces of magnesium in a blue solution
   B brown pieces of copper-coated magnesium in a blue solution
   C brown pieces of copper-coated magnesium in a colourless solution
   D grey pieces of magnesium in a colourless solution.

2. Which of the following occurs when copper metal is added to dilute sulphuric acid?
   A Hydrogen gas is produced.
   B Hydrogen and sulphur dioxide are produced.
   C Sulphur dioxide gas is produced.
   D There is no reaction.

3. An element called radikium has just been discovered. It is found to have a standard electrode potential of + 2.95. Where, in the electrochemical series, will you place this new element?
   A between aluminium and zinc
   B between lead and hydrogen
   C between hydrogen and copper
   D below silver.

4. W, X and Y are three metals. Element W does not react with cold water or steam. Element Y reacts with steam and its oxide is reduced by element X. The order in which they will appear in the reactivity series is:
   A WYX
   B WXY
   C XYW
   D YXW

5. What will be the products formed when zinc nitrate is heated?
   A zinc nitrate and oxygen
   B zinc oxide and nitrogen dioxide
   C zinc oxide, nitrogen dioxide and oxygen
   D zinc, nitrogen dioxide and oxygen

6. Which of the following is a list of compounds that will not decompose when heated by a bunsen flame?
   A K_2CO_3, Na_2CO_3, KOH
   B K_2CO_3, Na_2CO_3, $CaCO_3$
   C K_2CO_3, Na_2CO_3, $Ca(OH)_2$
   D K_2CO_3, Na_2CO_3, Li_2CO_3

7. Which of the following mixtures would you use to prepare hydrogen gas?
   A copper and dilute nitric acid
   B copper and concentrated sulphuric acid
   C magnesium and dilute sulphuric acid
   D zinc and concentrated sulphuric acid.

8. Which of the following elements reacts very slowly with cold water but readily with steam?
   A calcium
   B magnesium
   C barium
   D lithium

9. Which of the following is a list of oxides that can be reduced by hydrogen gas?
   A Fe_2O_3, PbO, CuO
   B MgO, PbO, CuO
   C Al_2O_3, MgO, CaO
   D Na_2O, K_2O, CaO

10. Which of the following is a list of compounds soluble in water?
    A Na_2CO_3, K_2CO_3, $CaCO_3$
    B Na_2CO_3, K_2CO_3, $Mg(OH)_2$
    C Na_2CO_3, KOH, $Mg(OH)_2$
    D Na_2CO_3, K_2CO_3, KOH

11. When heated, which of the following will decompose steam to form hydrogen?
    A copper
    B iron
    C copper (II) oxide
    D magnesium oxide

12. When heated, which of the following oxides can be reduced to its metal by hydrogen?
    A MgO
    B Al_2O_3
    C CaO
    D Fe_2O_3

13. Which one of the following metals does not react with any diluted acid to give hydrogen?
    A zinc
    B copper
    C magnesium
    D aluminium

14. Which of the following statement about hydrogen is incorrect?
    A It is the least dense substance known.
    B It forms stable +1 ions.
    C It is the most abundant element in the universe.
    D It is very soluble in water.

15. Use the electrochemical series to predict what will happen when the following substances are mixed. Write equations to represent each reaction that occurs.
    a copper and aqueous zinc sulphate
    b magnesium and dilute hydrochloric acid
    c iron nails in aqueous lead(II) nitrate
    d zinc and aqueous copper(II) sulphate
    e magnesium and iron(II) sulphate
    f lead and dilute sulphuric acid

16. This question concerns the metals copper, lead, sodium, magnesium and aluminium.
    a Which metal(s) will not react with dilute acids?
    b Which metal(s) will not react with cold water or steam?
    c Which metal(s) will react violently with cold water?
    d Which metal(s) will react with steam but not with cold water?
    e Which metal(s) have oxides that can be reduced by hydrogen gas?

17. W, X, Y and Z are all metals. Study the following information and answer the questions numbered a–d below.
    W reacts with steam.
    The nitrate of X decomposes to give the oxide, nitrogen dioxide gas and oxygen gas. X does not react with steam.
    The code of X is reduced by Y.
    Z reacts violently with cold water.
    a Which metal would you think will have a soluble carbonate?
    b Will there be any reaction when W is added to an aqueous salt of Z? If so, write an equation for the reaction.
    c Will there be any reaction when W is added to any aqueous solution of X? If so, write an equation for the reaction.
    d Arrange the metals in decreasing order of reactivity.

17 Electrolysis

Consider the following electrical circuit.

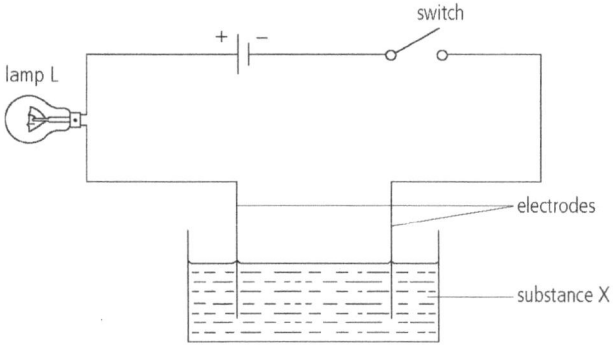

When the switch is closed, the lamp will light if:
- substance X is any metal, for example, copper, zinc or a substance such as graphite. These substances are **good conductors** of electricity;

or if:
- substance X is (a) a molten ionic compound, (b) an aqueous ionic compound, or (c) an aqueous solution of a covalent compound that ionises when dissolved in water. These substances are called electrolytes.

The lamp will not light if:
- substance X is a plastic, polystyrene or a non-metal such as sulphur. Most non-metals are non-conductors of electricity.

An electrolyte is any substance that will conduct an electric current when molten or in aqueous solution, but not when solid, for example, any ionic compound such as sodium chloride.

Some covalent compounds that produce ions in aqueous solution and are also electrolytes include: hydrogen chloride, hydrogen bromide, sulphuric acid and nitric acid.

Difference between metallic and electrolytic conduction

Metals conduct electricity by a movement of electrons through the metallic structure. Thus, solid metals can conduct electricity. Electrolytes conduct electricity because of the ability of positive and negative ions to move in aqueous solutions and molten compounds. They are unable to conduct electricity when solid because the ions are largely immobile due to strong forces of attraction. These forces are considerably reduced in aqueous solutions and in the molten compounds, giving the ions greater mobility.

Strong and weak electrolytes

Electrolytes that are almost completely ionised in aqueous solution are strong electrolytes, for example, an ionic compound, the mineral acids and the alkalis.

Weak electrolytes are ones which ionise to a small extent, for example, ethanoic acid or aqueous ammonia. Water is an extremely weak electrolyte.

The electrolytic process

Electrolysis can be defined as the passage of an electric current through an electrolyte with decomposition at the electrodes. The **electrodes** are the poles that take the current into, and out of, the electrolyte. The positive electrode is called the **anode** (+) and the negative one the **cathode** (−).

A generalised electrolytic cell is shown below.

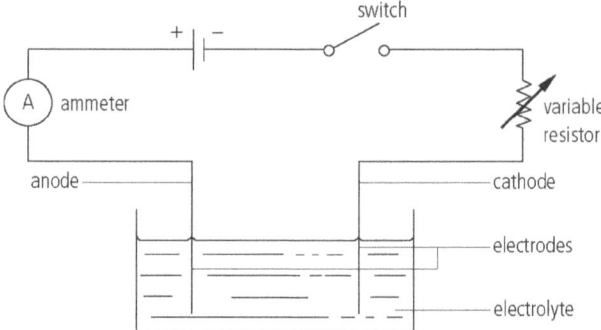

A generalised account of electrolysis

As the current is switched on, the ions migrate towards the electrodes. Positive ions move towards the negative cathode. For this reason, they are called cations. Negative ions move towards the positive anode. They are called anions.

At the electrodes the ions are discharged to produce neutral molecules. Positive ions accept electrons from the cathode and are discharged. The positive ions are being reduced. The **cathode** therefore is a **reducing agent**. Negative ions give up electrons to the **anode** and are therefore oxidised. The **anode** is therefore an **oxidising agent**.

$M^{z+} + ze \rightarrow M$

$N^{y-} \rightarrow N + ye$

As a result of the discharge of ions, there may be changes in the acidity or alkalinity of the solution.

Ions removed	H^+	OH^-	H^+ and OH^-
Change in acidity	Acidity decreases	Acidity increases	Acidity constant

When choosing electrodes keep in mind that the electrodes must not react with the electrolytes or with the products of electrolysis. Common electrodes are platinum or graphite.

Factors influencing discharge of ions at the electrodes

If there is more than one type of ion, which type of ion will be discharged at an electrode? The following will give the answer.
1. The main factor is the position of the ion in the electrochemical series.
2. Thus, the concentration of any ion may promote its discharge. In dilute halide solutions, OH^- ions are discharged producing oxygen. In concentrated halide solutions, the halide ions are mostly discharged because of their much greater concentration.
3. The third factor is the type of electrode used. See electrolysis of aqueous copper sulphate and the manufacture of sodium hydroxide using a mercury cathode. Na^+ ions are discharged instead of H^+ ions.

At the cathode

The positive ion that is lower down in the E.C.S. will accept electrons more easily and will be discharged in preference to the one above it.

K^+ Na^+ Ca^{2+} Mg^{2+} Al^{3+} Zn^{2+} Fe^{2+} Pb^{2+} H^+ Cu^{2+} Ag^+ $\longrightarrow$
Increasing ease of discharge

At the anode

The negative ion that is higher up in the E.C.S. will lose electrons more readily and will be discharged in preference to the one above it.

Electrode used including ions	Electrode	Electrode reactions including products	Change in acidity/ concentration of electrolyte
Fused lead(II) bromide: Pb^{2+}, Br^-	Anode: carbon Cathode: carbon or platinum	Anode: $2Br^- \rightarrow Br_2(g) + 2e$ Bromine is produced. Cathode: $Pb^{2+} + 2e \rightarrow Pb(l)$ Lead is produced.	None
Concentrated hydrochloric acid: H^+, Cl^-, OH^-	Anode: carbon Cathode: carbon or platinum	Anode: $2Cl^-(aq) \rightarrow Cl_2(g) + 2e$ Chlorine gas is produced. Cathode: $2H^+(aq) + 2e \rightarrow H_2(g)$ Hydrogen gas is produced.	Acidity decreases
Dilute sulphuric acid: H^+, SO_4^{2-}, OH^-	Anode: platinum Cathode: platinum	Anode: $4OH^-(aq) \rightarrow 2H_2O(l) + O_2(g) + 4e$ Cathode: $2H^+(aq) + 2e \rightarrow H_2(g)$	None
Dilute aqueous sodium chloride: Na^+, Cl^-, H^+, OH^-	Anode: carbon Cathode: carbon or platinum	Anode: $4OH^-(aq) \rightarrow 2H_2O(g) + O_2(g) + 4e$ Oxygen gas is produced. Cathode: $2H^+(aq) + 2e \rightarrow H_2$ Hydrogen is produced.	None
Concentrated aqueous solution of sodium chloride: Na^+, Cl^-, H^+, OH^-	Anode: carbon Cathode: carbon or platinum	Anode: $2Cl^-(aq) \rightarrow Cl_2(g) + 2e$ Chlorine gas is produced. Cathode: $2H^+(aq) + 2e \rightarrow H_2(g)$ Hydrogen gas is produced.	Acidity decreases
Copper(II) sulphate: Cu^{2+}, SO_4^{2-}, H^+, OH^-	Anode: platinum Cathode: platinum or copper	Anode: $4OH^-(aq) \rightarrow 2H_2O(l) + O_2(g) + 4e$ Oxygen gas is produced. Cathode: $Cu^{2+}(aq) + 2e \rightarrow Cu(s)$ Copper is deposited.	Acidity increases
Copper(II) sulphate	Anode: copper Cathode: platinum or copper	Anode: $Cu(s) \rightarrow Cu^{2+}(aq) + 2e$ Copper dissolves from anode. Cathode: $Cu^{2+}(aq) + 2e \rightarrow Cu(s)$ Copper is deposited.	**Note**: Anode decreases in mass and cathode increases.

←OH⁻ I⁻ Br⁻ Cl⁻ SO₄²⁻
Increasing ease of discharge

In aqueous solutions, OH⁻ will always be discharged except when the solution is a concentrated halide solution, for example, a concentrated solution of hydrochloric acid, sodium chloride, or any halide compound.

The table on page 38 gives specific examples of electrolysis.

Uses of electrolysis

Electroplating
Electrolysis is used to form a thin metal coating on the surface of an object, for example, jewellery or cans.

Metal and non-metal extractions
The DOWNS process is a procedure used to produce sodium. Molten sodium chloride is electrolysed between a graphite anode and iron cathode.

Electro-refining
Metals exist in mixtures with other substance. We can use electrolysis to purify metals such as copper.
Pure copper: $Cu^{2+}(aq) + 2e^- \rightarrow Cu(s)$
Impure copper: $Cu(s) \rightarrow 2e^- \rightarrow Cu^{2+}(aq)$

Pure copper accumulates on the copper strip that forms the cathode. The impurities from the anode drop to the bottom of the cell. Impure copper is made the anode in a electrolytic cell. The cell uses a pure strip of copper as the cathode and aqueous copper sulphate as the electrolyte. Other elements extracted by electrolysis are Al, Cl and Na.

Questions

1. During the electrolysis of a dilute solution of sodium chloride using inert electrodes, the gas produced at the anode will most likely:
   A bleach litmus **B** turn lime water cloudy
   C relight a glowing splint
   D explode when a lighted splint is applied.

2. When copper(II) sulphate solution is electrolysed using copper electrodes, the reactions going on at the electrodes can be represented by:

Anode (+)	Cathode (−)
A $4OH^-(aq) \rightarrow 2H_2O(l) + O_2(g) + 4e$	$Cu^{2+}(aq) + 2e \rightarrow Cu(s)$
B $Cu(s) \rightarrow Cu^{2+}(aq) + 2e$	$Cu^{2+}(aq) + 2e \rightarrow Cu(s)$
C $SO_4^{2-}(aq) \rightarrow SO_2(g) + O_2(g) + 2e$	$Cu^{2+}(aq) + 2e \rightarrow Cu(s)$
D $Cu^{2+}(aq) + 2e \rightarrow Cu(s)$	$Cu(s) \rightarrow Cu^{2+}(aq) + 2e$

3. An electrolyte conducts electricity through the movement of:
   A positive ions   **C** positive and negative ions
   B negative ions   **D** electrons.

4. Ethanoic acid is considered to be a weak electrolyte because it:
   A is a covalent compound
   B is only slightly ionised in aqueous solution
   C is composed of immobile ions
   D reacts slowly with metals.

The apparatus below concerns questions 5 and 6.

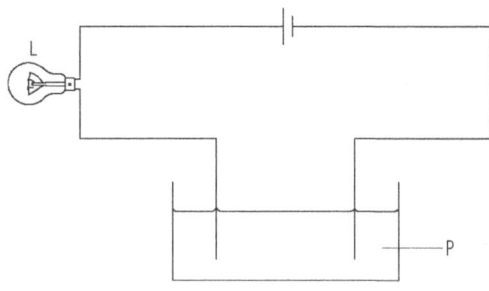

5. The lamp will not light if P is:
   A a sugar solution
   B aqueous sodium chloride
   C molten sodium chloride
   D mercury.

6. The lamp will light the brightest when P is:
   A aqueous ammonia
   B aqueous ethanoic acid
   C aqueous sulphuric acid
   D carbonic acid.

7. Copper(II) sulphate solution can be electrolysed using platinum electrodes.
   a. Which ions are present in the solution?
   b. Which ions go to the (i) anode (ii) cathode?
   c. Which ions will be discharged at the (i) anode (ii) cathode? Write equations for the reactions.
   d. What happens to the acidity of the solution as electrolysis proceeds?
   e. What changes would there be in questions **c** and **d** if the anode were copper, not platinum?
   f. What is the industrial importance of **e**?

8. A concentrated solution of sodium chloride is electrolysed using carbon electrodes.
   a. Which ions are present in the solution?
   b. Which ions will be attracted to the (i) anode (ii) cathode?
   c. Which type of ion will be discharged at each electrode? Write equations for the reactions.
   d. What changes occur in the acidity of the solution?
   e. What changes will there be in questions **c** and **d** if the cathode were mercury, not carbon?
   f. What is the industrial importance of **e**?

18 Calculations involving electrolysis

Faraday's laws of electrolysis

Faraday stated that the quantity of a substance deposited or liberated during electrolysis depends on:
a the magnitude of the current (ampere)
b the time for which it flows
c the charge on the ion.

Quantity of electricity is measured in coulombs (C). One coulomb is the quantity of electricity when one ampere flows for one second.

$$\text{Quantity (Q)} = \text{Current (I)} \times \text{Time (t)}$$
$$\text{coulombs} \quad\quad \text{ampere} \quad\quad \text{seconds}$$

The quantity of electricity produced when 2.00 amperes flow for 6 minutes is $2.00 \times 6.00 \times 60.0 = 720$ C.

The Faraday constant is taken to be approximately 96 500 C, and is said to supply one mole of electrons.

Thus, the Faraday constant will discharge one mole of an ion with one charge.

$$M^+ + e \rightarrow M \text{ or } N^- \rightarrow N + e$$

The Faraday constant will discharge ½ mole of ions with 2 charges and ⅓ mole of ions with 3 charges.

The Faraday constant is needed to discharge one mole of Na^+. Twice the Faraday constant is needed to discharge one mole of copper ions and three times the Faraday constant is needed to discharge one mole of aluminium ions.

Twice the Faraday constant is needed to produce one mole of hydrogen molecules:

$$2H^+(aq) + 2e \rightarrow H_2(g)$$

Sample calculations

1 What mass of copper will be deposited when 5.00 amperes flow for 193 seconds through an aqueous copper(II) compound?
(R.A.M. of copper = 64, F = 96 500 C)

Quantity of electricity flowing $= 5.00 \times 193$
$= 965$ C

$$Cu^{2+}(aq) + 2e \rightarrow Cu(s)$$

Twice the Faraday constant will deposit one mole of Cu (64 g), i.e. $2 \times 96\ 500$ C of electricity will deposit 64.0 g of Cu.

975 C of electricity will deposit:

$$64.0 \times \frac{965}{2 \times 96\ 500}$$

$= 0.320$ g

2 0.200 Faraday is passed through an aqueous solution of sulphuric acid.
a Write equations to show what is liberated at each electrode.
b Calculate the volume of gas liberated at each electrode. Then find the ratio of oxygen liberated to hydrogen liberated (molar volume at room temperature and pressure is 24 dm³).

a Anode(+)
$4OH^-(aq) \rightarrow 2H_2O(l) + O_2(g) + 4e$

Cathode (−)
$2H^+(aq) + 2e \rightarrow H_2(g)$

b Anode(+)
Four times the Faraday constant will liberate one mole of oxygen.

One-fifth of the Faraday constant will liberate:

$\frac{1 \times 0.200}{4}$

= 0.0500 mole of oxygen
One mole of oxygen at r.t.p. occupies 24 dm³
0.0500 mole of oxygen at r.t.p. occupies:
24×0.0500
= 1.20 dm³
= 1 200 cm³

Cathode (−)
Twice the Faraday constant will liberate one mole of hydrogen, i.e. 24 dm³ hydrogen at r.t.p.

So, one-fifth of the Faraday constant will liberate:

$\frac{24 \times 0.200}{2}$ dm³

= 2.40 dm³
= 2 400 cm³

Thus, the ratio of oxygen to hydrogen is 1 : 2.

3 When 2.00 amperes were passed through a solution of a copper salt for 965 seconds, 0.64 g of copper was deposited at the cathode. What is the charge on the copper ion?
(Faraday constant = 96 500 C, R.A.M. of copper = 64)

Quantity of electricity used $= 2.00 \times 965$ C
$= 1\ 930$ C

0.64 g of copper was liberated by 1 930 C
64 g of copper (1 mole) will be liberated by:

$1\ 930 \times \frac{64}{0.64}$

= 193 000 C
= twice the Faraday constant.
The charge on the copper ion is + 2.

Questions

1. The Faraday constant will liberate:
   A 27 g of aluminium and 24 g of magnesium
   B 27 g of aluminium and 12 g of magnesium
   C 13.5 g of aluminium and 12 g of magnesium
   D 9 g of aluminium and 12 g of magnesium.

2. The volume, in litres, of chlorine gas liberated by the Faraday constant at room temperature and pressure is:
   A 5.6   B 6   C 12   D 24

3. Consider the following equation:
   $2O^{2-} \rightarrow O_2 + 4e$
   The volume of oxygen gas, in litres, produced at the anode at room temperature and pressure when the Faraday constant is passed through a solution of aluminium oxide in cryolite, will be:
   A 5.6   B 6   C 12   D 24

4. A current of 5 amperes is passed through an aqueous solution of copper(II) sulphate for 1 930 seconds. The mass, in grams, of copper deposited will be:
   A 3.2   B 6.4   C 32   D 64

5. When a current of 2.5 amperes was passed through an aqueous solution for 193 seconds, 0.22 g of metal was deposited on the cathode. If the relative atomic mass of the metal is 88, what is the charge on the ion?
   A +1   B +2   C −1   D −2

6. 120 cm³ of oxygen, measured at room temperature and pressure, was obtained at the anode when dilute sulphuric acid was electrolysed between platinum electrodes. If the current passed was 1 ampere, for how long (in seconds) was the electric current passed?
   A 193   B 482.5   C 965   D 1 930

7. The Faraday constant at room temperature and pressure will produce 12 litres of:
   I oxygen
   II hydrogen
   III chlorine.
   A I, II and III   C II and III only
   B I and II only   D III only
   (Molar volume at room temperature and pressure is 24 litres.)

8. One-tenth of the Faraday constant is passed through solutions of copper(II) sulphate and silver nitrate arranged in series. The masses of copper and silver deposited will be:

	Mass of copper (g)	Mass of silver (g)
A	3.2	5.4
B	3.2	10.8
C	3.2	108.0
D	6.4	10.8

9. The Faraday constant supplies:
   I 1 mole of electrons
   II 96 500 C of electricity
   III 6.02×10^{23} electrons.
   A I, II and III   C II and III only
   B I and II only   D I only

10. A current of 3 amperes is passed through an aqueous salt solution for 2 minutes. The number of coulombs passed is:
    A 6   B 180   C 360   D 96 500

11. A current of 10 amperes was passed through a dilute solution of sulphuric acid for 193 seconds using platinum electrodes.
    a What was the quantity of electricity used in the experiment (i) in coulombs (ii) in terms of the Faraday constant?
    b Which gas would be produced at (i) the anode (ii) the cathode?
    c Write equations to represent (i) the anodic reaction (ii) the cathodic reaction.
    d Calculate the volume of each gas produced at (i) the anode (ii) the cathode at room temperature and pressure. (Faraday constant = 96 500 C)

12. A current of 2 amperes was passed through a moderately concentrated solution of sodium chloride for 482.5 seconds using graphite electrodes.
    a What was the quantity of electricity used in the experiment (i) in coulombs (ii) in terms of the Faraday constant?
    b Which gas is produced at (i) the anode (ii) the cathode?
    c Calculate the volume of gas produced at (i) the anode (ii) the cathode at room temperature and pressure.
    d How can these gases be identified?
    e The volume of gas produced at the anode was 100 cm³. How does this compare with your answer in c(i)? Account for any difference between the two.

13. Calculate the masses of:
    a copper deposited by passing one ampere through an aqueous copper(II) salt for 193 seconds
    b silver deposited by passing a current of two amperes through aqueous silver nitrate for 96.5 seconds
    c oxygen liberated by 965 coulombs of electricity from aqueous sodium hydroxide
    d hydrogen liberated by 965 C of electricity from aqueous sodium hydroxide.

19 Energy

Forms of energy

There are several forms of energy. The most important forms are: chemical, heat, electrical, mechanical and sound energy. These forms of energy can be converted from one form into another. For example: the steam engine uses chemical energy from coal to produce heat energy in the form of steam. This heat energy is then converted mainly into mechanical energy.

In the whistling kettle, chemical energy is used to produce heat energy, some of which is then converted to sound energy.

The food we eat contains chemical energy which is converted to heat energy for warmth, to mechanical energy in our muscles, and into electrical energy in our nerve impulses.

Major energy sources

Our main energy sources today are the fossil fuels – coal, oil and natural gas. Wood is also used in some places. The ultimate source of all this energy is the sun. Some other sources of energy used today are nuclear and hydroelectric energy.

Alternative sources of energy

The fossil fuels, especially oil and natural gas, are being used up at a very fast rate and, at present consumption levels, will run out at some time in the next century. The reserves of coal are greater and are expected to last a few centuries more. However, these fuels are all non-renewable, so, if humans are to survive, alternative energy sources have to be developed.

One of the possible major sources of energy is **nuclear fission**. However, popular pressure against this form of energy has slowed down its development. There are two objections to the use of this kind of energy, namely: it is dangerous to handle nuclear fuel, and it is a problem to safely dispose of the toxic waste.

The source of the sun's energy is **nuclear fusion**. Research is being carried out in this field but success is quite a far way off.

Other sources of energy being developed are geothermal, wind, solar, biogas, gasohol and tidal energy.

Gasohol has wide application in Brazil, where alcohol is produced and mixed with gasoline to provide fuel for motor cars.

Biogas seeks to use organic matter such as animal waste to generate combustible gases.

Wood, peat and charcoal as fuels

Many Caribbean countries use wood and charcoal as fuels, particularly in homes. Charcoal is produced by the controlled burning of wood. This can have serious consequences for the environment as deforestation causes the loss of soil fertility, among other things. There is need for the control of deforestation.

Wood burns at a much faster rate than charcoal and peat. Peat is formed in the process of converting vegetation to coal. Peat is not used much in the Caribbean, although Jamaica is now planning to utilise its peat resources. There is some controversy over this decision as experts differ in their opinions over the possible environmental effects. The energy values of wood, peat and coal are shown below. These values are for 1 kg of material.

Fuel	Energy value per kg(J)
Wood	3×10^6
Peat	5×10^6 to 6×10^6
Coal	6×10^6 to 7×10^6

Questions

1. What are the main sources of energy used in your country today?
2. What other energy resources are being developed in your country?
3. Write a short account on each of the following: (a) biogas (b) solar energy (c) gasohol. Are any of the above, viable alternatives to fossil fuel in your country?
4. Name two fossil fuels. How long can humans hope to have these fuels for their use? If you were appointed Minister of Energy in your country, what are some of the things you would implement to conserve energy?
5. Write a short account of the suitability of wood, peat and charcoal as fuels. You may wish to compare their energy values and rates of combustion.
6. What is the source of the sun's energy? Can we duplicate this source of energy on earth? Comment on the problems being experienced in the research of this source of energy.
7. Today nuclear energy is produced by nuclear fission. Briefly explain what is meant by 'nuclear fission'. Explain some of the problems being encountered by the generation of this kind of energy.

20 Chemical energetics

Energy changes during chemical reactions

All compounds have a certain amount of energy stored in them. This is referred to as the 'energy content' of the substance. This energy is stored mainly in the form of bonds. During a chemical reaction, bonds are broken and new ones are formed. The breaking of bonds requires energy and is therefore an **endothermic process**, i.e. energy is absorbed. The formation of bonds releases energy to the surroundings and is therefore an **exothermic process**.

A reaction in which energy is released to the surroundings (mainly as heat) is called an exothermic reaction.

The change in energy content is the difference between the energy content of the product and the energy content of the reactant. This is referred to as ΔH.

$\Delta H = H_{Products} - H_{Reactants}$, H represents the energy content of the product and reactant respectively.

In an exothermic reaction, the energy content of the product will be less than that of the reactants. ΔH will therefore have a negative value. In an endothermic reaction, the product will have a higher energy content that the reactants. ΔH will therefore have a positive value. These can be represented graphically. The graphs are called energy profile diagrams.

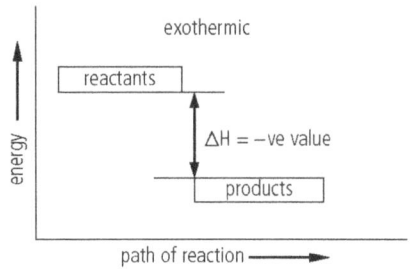

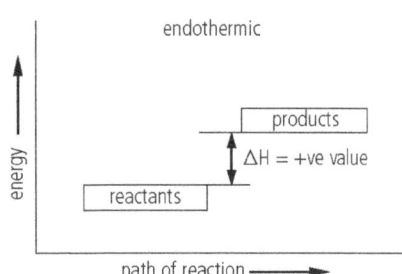

Some examples of endothermic processes are:
a the dissolving of ammonium chloride in water
b the dissolving of potassium nitrate in water.

In endothermic processes, the container will become cool, showing that heat is being absorbed from the surroundings.

Some examples of exothermic processes are:
a reacting an acid with an alkali
b the precipitation of barium sulphate
c mixing concentrated sulphuric acid and water.

In exothermic processes, the container will become warm or hot, showing that energy is given out to the surroundings. There are many heats of reactions, for example, the heats of neutralisation, combustion, precipitation and solution. These can all be referred to as molar heats of reactions if molar quantities are involved in the reaction.

The molar heat of neutralisation of an acid is the heat change when one mole of hydrogen ions is neutralised by hydroxide ions from an alkali. The molar heat of solution is the heat evolved or absorbed when one mole of a solute forms an infinitely dilute solution. The heat of neutralisation of a strong acid and alkali can be found as follows:

Hydrochloric acid and sodium hydroxide solutions should both be exposed to room temperature so that they acquire this temperature. Exactly 50.0 cm³ of 2.00 mol dm⁻³ hydrochloric acid is placed in a polystyrene cup. The temperature of this solution is taken using a thermometer than can read to an accuracy of 0.2 °C. Exactly 50.0 cm³ of 2.00 mol dm⁻³ sodium hydroxide solution is then added while stirring constantly. The highest temperature reached is then recorded. The molar heat of solution can be calculated. The following is a sample calculation:

Original temperature of acid solution = 25.2 °C
Highest temperature recorded = 38.0 °C
Temperature rise = 12.8 °C

Number of moles of acid used $= \dfrac{2.00 \times 50.0}{1\,000}$

$= 0.100$ mole

Heat evolved from reaction
(ignoring mass of solutes and heat
lost to container and surroundings) $= 100.0 \times 4.2 \ldots$
$\ldots \times 12.8$ J

This amount of heat was produced by neutralising 0.100 mole of acid.

The molar heat of neutralisation $= \dfrac{100.0 \times 4.2 \times 12.8}{0.100}$

$= -53.8$ kJ mole⁻¹

The molar heat of neutralisation of a strong acid with an alkali is about −57.3 kJ. Why is the above figure less?

The following experiment can be used to find the approximate heat of combustion for an alcohol.

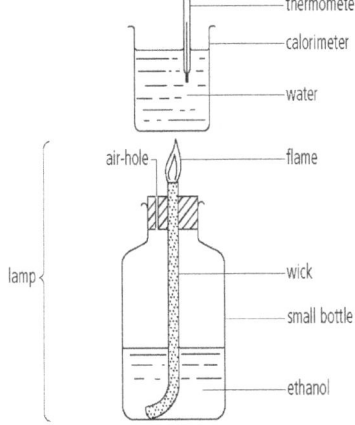

The mass of the lamp is found before the wick is lit. The temperature of the water is also recorded. The temperature is then allowed to rise about 30 °C after which the lamp is extinguished and reweighed. The heat of combustion can then be calculated.

Mass of water = 100.00 g
Original mass of lamp = 25.492 g
Original temperature of water = 25 °C
Final mass of lamp = 25.446 g
Mass of ethanol burnt = 0.46 g
Final temperature = 55 °C
Temperature rise = 30 °C
Heat gained by water = 100 × 4.2 × 30 J
= 12 600 J

So, 0.46 g of ethanol produced 12 600 J
46 g of ethanol produced 1 260 000 J = 1 260 kJ
The approximate molar heat of combustion of ethanol is therefore: 1 260 kJ mole^{-1} (rounded to 1 300 kJ for significant figures).

Questions

1. During a chemical reaction bond breaking and bond formation takes place. Which of the following is true?
   A Bond breaking requires energy.
   B Energy is absorbed when bonds are formed.
   C Bond breaking is an exothermic process.
   D There is no net energy change when the two processes take place.

2. In an exothermic reaction:
   A the total energy content of the products is greater than that of the reactants
   B the total energy content of the products is less than that of the reactants
   C the total energy content of the products is equal to that of the reactants
   D the change in heat content is usually assigned a positive value.

3. When ammonium chloride is dissolved in water, the test tube becomes cold. This indicates that:
   A an endothermic process has occurred
   B an exothermic process has occurred
   C the ammonium chloride has released heat energy to the surroundings
   D the heat content of ammonium chloride is small.

4. When concentrated sulphuric acid is mixed with water in a beaker, the beaker becomes hot. This is because:
   A an endothermic process has occurred
   B an exothermic process has occurred
   C the sulphuric acid has absorbed a lot of heat energy from the surroundings
   D the heat content of sulphuric acid is very high.

5. The heat evolved when one mole of hydrochloric acid is neutralised by an alkali is greater than that evolved when one mole of ethanol acid is neutralised by an alkali. This is because:
   A the energy content of hydrochloric acid is greater than that of ethanoic acid
   B the energy content of ethanoic acid is greater than that of hydrochloric acid
   C the energy needed to ionise the ethanoic acid molecules is greater than that needed to ionise hydrochloric acid molecules
   D the energy needed to ionise hydrochloric acid is greater than that needed for ethanoic acid.

6. When 4 g of sodium hydroxide was dissolved in 100 cm^3 of water, the temperature of the water rose from 25 °C to 30 °C. The heat in joules given out to the surroundings when the temperature of the solution cools down to room temperature will be:
   A 500 J   B 2 100 J   C 2 500 J   D 8 400 J
   (The specific heat capacity of water is 4.2 J °C^{-1} g^{-1})

7. 50 cm^3 of molar hydrochloric acid is mixed with 50 cm^3 of molar sodium hydroxide in a plastic beaker. There is a temperature rise of 6.5 °C. Both solutions were at room temperature at the start of the experiment.
   a Was the reaction exothermic or endothermic?
   b How many moles of hydrochloric acid were used in the experiment?
   c Calculate the heat, in joules, given out to the surroundings when the mixture cools down to room temperature.
   d Use your results from c to find the molar heat of neutralisation for the reaction.
   e The value given in a data book for the molar heat of neutralisation of a strong acid by an alkali is −57.3 kJ.
   How will your result in d compare with this? Explain any differences in value.

21 Equilibria

Example 1

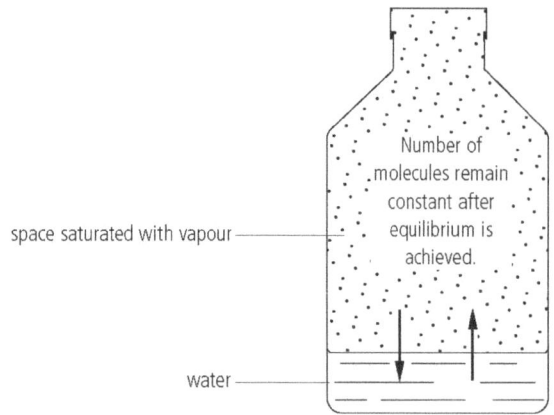

Observe some water in a closed container. After a while, the air above the water will become saturated with vapour due to evaporation. At this point, the number of particles in the vapour and the liquid states will be constant. This does not mean that evaporation has stopped. Evaporation continues, but the rate of evaporation is equal to the rate of condensation. The system is now said to be in dynamic equilibrium. Two opposing processes are going on at the same rate, causing the amount of liquid and vapour to be constant at a particular temperature. This equilibrium can be attained only in a closed system, i.e. one in which no matter can enter or leave.

Example 2

When calcium carbonate is heated, it decomposes to calcium oxide and carbon dioxide. Ordinarily, the gas will escape to the atmosphere and the process will go to completion. However, if the calcium carbonate is being heated in a closed test tube at a fixed temperature, the system will attain a dynamic chemical equilibrium. At first, calcium carbonate will decompose to give calcium oxide and carbon dioxide. These two substances will then react to give calcium carbonate. This backward process will at first be very slow, increasing in rate as the concentrations of calcium oxide and carbon dioxide increase. On the other hand, the forward reaction will be slowing down as the concentration of calcium carbonate decreases. There will come a time when the rate of the forward reaction is equal to the rate of the backward reaction. At this point the system is said to have attained a dynamic chemical equilibrium. Both reversible processes are still going on but at the same rate. The amount of carbon dioxide, calcium oxide and calcium carbonate will therefore remain constant.

$$CaCO_3(s) \rightleftharpoons CaO(s) + CO_2(g)$$

Le Chatelier's principle

Le Chatelier's principle states that if a system is in chemical equilibrium and one of the factors involved in the equilibrium, namely pressure, temperature or concentration, is altered, then the system will react in such a way that will oppose this change.

Thus, if the temperature of a system in chemical equilibrium is raised, the system will do something that will use up heat and thus lower the temperature, though the temperature may not necessarily decrease to what it was at the start.

Haber process

Starting materials: nitrogen from the air, hydrogen obtained from petroleum and steam:

$N_2(g) + 3H_2(g) \rightleftharpoons 2HN_3(g)$ ΔH = –ve value

The forward reaction is exothermic and will therefore be favoured by a low temperature. However, a compromise temperature of 450–500 °C is used because the rate of the reaction will be too slow below this.

In this reaction 4 volumes of reactants are giving 2 volumes of product. This reaction will therefore be favoured by high pressure. The pressure used is between 200 and 500 atmospheres.

A catalyst is also used to speed up the reaction and make the operating temperature lower. This catalyst is finely divided iron. The ammonia is separated from the unreacted gases by liquefaction or by dissolving in water. The unreacted nitrogen and hydrogen are recycled.

Contact process

Starting materials: sulphur dioxide obtained from sulphur and iron pyrites, and oxygen from the air:

$2SO_2(g) + O_2(g) \rightleftharpoons 2SO_3(g)$ ΔH = –ve

Since the forward reaction is exothermic, it will be favoured by a low temperature. However, a temperature of 450–500 °C is used as the process will be too slow otherwise. Since the reaction proceeds with a decease in volume, high pressure will favour the forward reaction. However, the reaction proceeds to over 90% yield at atmospheric pressure, so high pressure, which is costly, is not used. A catalyst, vanadium(V) oxide, is used to speed up the reaction. The SO_3 is dissolved in concentrated H_2SO_4, as dissolving in water results in a fog of sulphuric acid being formed.

Summary

a Exothermic reaction is favoured by a low temperature.
b Endothermic reaction is favoured by a high temperature.
c A reaction that proceeds with an increase in volume is favoured by a low pressure.
d A reaction that proceeds with a reduction in volume is favoured by a high pressure.
e Increasing the concentration of reactants generally favours the forward reaction.

Questions

1 Which of the following systems attain a position of equilibrium?
 A Undissolved copper(II) sulphate in copper(II) solution.
 B A stoppered bottle of bromine.
 C An open pot of boiling water.
 D The heating of calcium carbonate in a stoppered test tube.

2 When a system attains a position of dynamic chemical equilibrium:
 A the reaction stops
 B the rate of the forward reaction is faster than the rate of the backward reaction
 C the rate of the forward reaction is slower than the rate of the backward reaction
 D the rate of the forward reaction is equal to the rate of the backward reaction.

3 The oxidation of ammonia to nitrogen monoxide is highly exothermic. This reaction will be favoured by:
 A low temperature
 B room temperature
 C moderately high temperature
 D very high temperature.

4 Ammonia is manufactured by the Haber process according to the equation:
 $N_2(g) + 3H_2(g) \rightleftharpoons 2NH_3(g)$
 The forward reaction will be favoured by:
 I low temperature
 II high pressure
 III increased concentration of nitrogen.
 A I, II and III
 B I and II only
 C II and III only
 D I only

5 The combination of sulphur dioxide and oxygen to give sulphur trioxide is exothermic. An increase in temperature will:
 A favour the formation of sulphur trioxide
 B favour the decomposition of sulphur trioxide
 C have no effect on the position of equilibrium
 D decrease the rate of both forward and backward reactions.

6 Hydrogen iodide decomposes according to the following equation:
 $2HI(g) \rightleftharpoons H_2(g) + I_2(g)$ $\Delta H = +ve$
 Which of the following factors will shift the position of equilibrium to the right?
 A decreasing the temperature
 B increasing the temperature
 C increasing the concentration of hydrogen iodide
 D using a catalyst.

7 Sodium hydroxide solution is added drop by drop to an aqueous solution of bromine until the orange colour disappears. The orange colour can now be restored by adding:
 A dilute hydrochloric acid
 B aqueous ammonia
 C water
 D sodium carbonate solution.

8 When radioactive lead(II) iodide was added to a saturated solution of ordinary lead(II) iodide, the solution became radioactive but the concentration of the lead(II) iodide solution remained constant. This shows that:
 A Radioactive lead(II) iodide is more soluble in water than ordinary lead(II) iodide.
 B There was a dynamic equilibrium between undissolved lead iodide and the solution.
 C Ordinary lead(II) iodide is more soluble in water when mixed with radioactive lead(II) iodide.
 D Lead(II) iodide is very soluble in water.

9 94 cm³ of an equilibrium mixture of N_2O_4 and NO_2 are placed in a syringe at atmospheric pressure. The pressure is doubled by placing a mass of 8 kg on the syringe. The new volume of the gases was not 47 cm³ as expected, but 42 cm³ instead.
 $N_2O_4(g) \rightleftharpoons 2NO_2(g)$
 The volume of gases decreased more than expected because:
 A some of the gases escaped from the syringe
 B NO_2 molecules combined to form N_2O_4 molecules
 C N_2O_4 molecules decomposed to give NO_2 molecules
 D the molecules of the gases became smaller with the increased pressure.

10 The experiment in question 9 shows that when pressure is increased:
 A The equilibrium shift is in the direction of the reaction that causes an increase in the number of molecules.
 B The equilibrium shift is in the direction of the reaction that causes a decrease in the number of molecules.
 C The equilibrium position is unaffected.
 D The molecules of gases become smaller.

22 Rate of reaction

The rate of a chemical reaction can be measured in terms of the rate of disappearance of the reactants or in terms of the rate of formation of the products. For example, consider the reaction between calcium carbonate and dilute hydrochloric acid. As carbon dioxide is produced, it can be allowed to escape to the atmosphere. The total mass of the flask will therefore decrease as the reaction proceeds and so the rate of the reaction can be measured in terms of the rate of decrease in the mass of the flask. The rate of formation of carbon dioxide can also be used as a measure of the rate of the reaction. The rate of a reaction is generally measured in moles per unit time, i.e. mol s^{-1}.

The rate of chemical reactions

The factors that affect the rate of chemical reactions are:
- concentration
- temperature
- surface area
- catalyst

Experiment to find out how changes in concentration affect the rate of a chemical reaction

Method | 40 g dm^{-3} sodium thiosulphate solution is placed in a conical flask and 2 mol dm^{-3} hydrochloric acid is added. The mixture is then swirled and the flask placed on a sheet of white paper with a cross marked on it. Start timing the reaction as soon as the hydrochloric acid is added. The time taken for the mark to disappear due to precipitated sulphur, should be noted. The experiment is repeated four times using the quantities shown in the table. The volume of thiosulphate is made up to 50 cm³ in each case, effectively diluting its concentration.

Number of experiment	Volume of HCl (cm³)	Volume of thiosulphate (cm³)	Volume of water (cm³)
1	5	50	0
2	5	40	10
3	5	30	20
4	5	20	30
5	5	10	40

Result | The time taken for the mark to disappear increases as the concentration of the thiosulphate decreases. Thus, the rate of chemical reaction decreases as the concentration of the reactants decreases.

Experiment to find out how temperature affects the rate of a chemical reaction

The above experiment can be repeated using the figures shown in the table below.

No. of experiment	Volume of HCl (cm³)	Volume of thio-sulphate (cm³)	Volume of water (cm³)	Temp. (°C)
1	5	10	40	30
2	5	10	40	40
3	5	10	40	50
4	5	10	40	60
5	5	10	40	70

Result | It will be observed that the rate of the reaction increases as the temperature increases.

Experiment to find out the effect of surface area on the rate of a chemical reaction

Look at the reaction between marble chips (calcium carbonate) and dilute hydrochloric acid.

$$CaCO_3(s) + 2HCl(aq) \rightarrow CaCl_2(aq) + H_2O(l) + CO_2(g)$$

The rate of reaction can be measured in terms of the loss of mass of the reaction vessel.

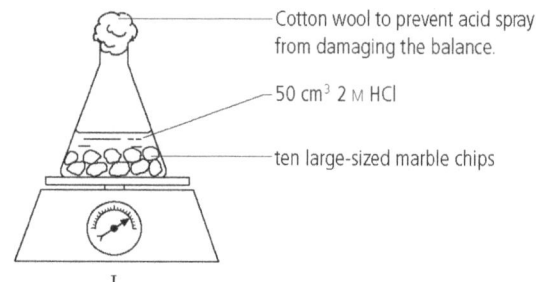

I

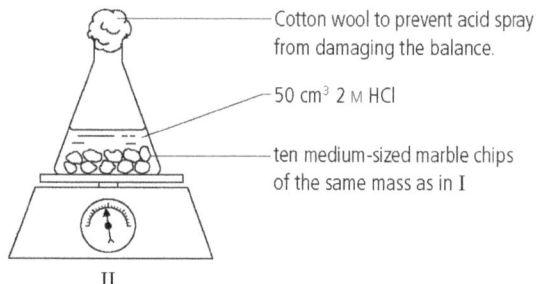

II

Result | The rate of reaction is faster with the smaller-sized marble chips.

Experiment to find out the effect of a catalyst on the rate of decomposition of hydrogen peroxide

Decomposition of hydrogen peroxide is very slow, as can be seen in Figure I below.

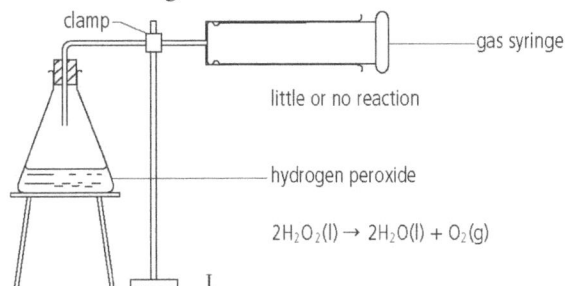

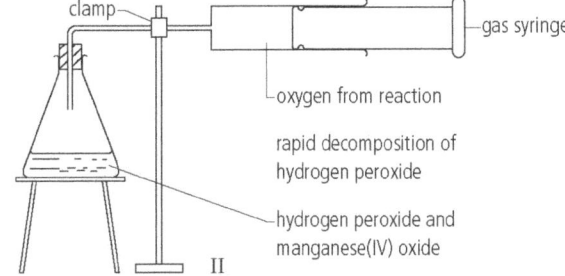

When manganese(IV) oxide is added to the hydrogen peroxide it decomposes very rapidly (see Figure II).

Reasons for the effects of various factors on rate of reaction

Chemical reactions take place as a result of collisions between reactant particles. Any factor that increases the rate of collisions will also increase the rate of a reaction.

Effect of concentration

Increasing the concentration of the reactants will increase the number of reacting particles, so increasing the number of collisions and also the rate of reaction.

Effect of temperature

Increasing the temperature increases the rate of movement of the reactant particles, so increasing the rate of collisions. The rate of reaction will therefore increase. Also, the increased temperature increases the number of collisions that have more than the minimum energy required to react – the activation energy; so the reaction rate increases still further.

Surface area and the rate of reaction

The surface area of a substance is the size of the surface exposed. A number of small pieces have a larger surface area than one larger piece of material.

If you have a larger piece of material, most of the particles are locked inside and cannot react until they are exposed. But if you have many small pieces, there are more exposed particles that can react immediately.

The smaller the particle size, the greater the exposed surface area, causing an increased number of collisions and an increase in the rate of reaction.

Effect of a catalyst

The catalyst remains unaltered, but causes a chemical reaction to go by another route that needs less energy, i.e. the activation energy is lowered. The activation energy is the amount of energy that reactant particles must have after collision in order to go on to the product. Since the catalyst lowers the activation energy, more reactant particles will have this activation energy and go on to the product. This causes an increase in the rate of reaction.

Questions

1. Sodium carbonate reacts with dilute hydrochloric acid to produce sodium chloride, water and carbon dioxide gas. The rate of the reaction can be followed by measuring the:
   I rate of formation of carbon dioxide using a gas syringe
   II rate of decrease in mass of the reacting vessel
   III time taken for a fixed mass of sodium carbonate to disappear.
   A I, II and III **C** II and III only
   B I and II only **D** I only

2. Marble chips are reacted with 50 cm³ of 2 M hydrochloric acid to produce carbon dioxide. Which of the following factors will not cause an increase in the rate of reaction?
   A Using 50 cm³ of 4 M HCl instead of 2 M HCl.
   B Crushing the marble chips into smaller pieces.
   C Using 100 cm³ of 2 M HCl instead of 50 cm³ of 2 M HCl.
   D Increasing the temperature.

3. In which of the following cases will oxygen be produced at the fastest rate?
   A Adding manganese(IV) oxide to a solution containing 1 cm³ of hydrogen peroxide and 49 cm³ of water at 40 °C.
   B Heating a solution containing 1 cm³ of hydrogen peroxide in 49 cm³ of water to 40 °C.
   C Heating a solution containing 2 cm³ of hydrogen peroxide in 48 cm³ of water.
   D Adding manganese(IV) oxide to a solution of 2 cm³ hydrogen peroxide in 48 cm³ of water.

4. A piece of zinc is reacted with 2 M sulphuric acid to produce hydrogen gas. Give three ways of increasing the rate of the reaction. Describe experiments you could do to show how the factors you have given affect the rate of reaction. Why do these factors increase the rate of reaction.

23 Metals and non-metals

The table below lists properties of metals and non-metals as well as their differences.

Metals	Non-metals
Are generally solids with high melting points and boiling points, except mercury which is a liquid at room temperature. The alkali metals also have low melting points.	Are usually liquids or gases at room temperature except carbon, phosphorus, sulphur and iodine.
Possess a lustre.	Do not possess a lustre (except graphite and diamond).
Are good conductors of heat and electricity.	Are poor conductors of heat and electricity, except graphite.
Are malleable (can be beaten into sheets), ductile (can be drawn into wires), possess high tensile strengths and generally have high densities.	Are not malleable or ductile, possess low tensile strengths and generally have low densities.
Form basic oxides and hydroxides, except those of zinc, aluminium and lead which are amphoteric.	Generally forms acidic oxides. Carbon monoxide, water and nitrogen oxide are neutral oxides.
Those above hydrogen in the E.C.S. react with dilute acids to produce hydrogen gas and salts.	Do not react with dilute acids.
Are electropositive, losing electrons to form positive ions.	Are generally electronegative, gaining electrons to form negative ions.
React only with non-metals to form ionic compounds.	React with metals to form ionic compounds and with non-metals to form covalent compounds.
Form ionic chlorides.	Form covalent chlorides.
Very electropositive metals form ionic hydrides.	Form covalent hydrides.

Explanation of some metallic properties

Metallic structure

In a metallic structure, the metals contribute their outermost electrons to form a common pool. The metallic ions formed will tend to repel each other, but are held together by the moving pool of electrons which are distributed throughout the metallic lattice. In some metals, for example alkali metals, the attraction is weak, resulting in low melting points. The weak attraction is due to the fact that the alkali metals' atoms can each contribute only one electron to the pool. Alkaline earth metals will therefore have a higher melting point. Transition metals, which can contribute electrons from their penultimate shell, will have the strongest metallic bonds and hence the highest melting points.

increasing strength of metallic bond →

alkali metals, alkaline earth metals, aluminium, transition metals →

increasing melting point, increasing tensile strength →

Because of the mobile electron cloud, metals can conduct heat and electricity. Their malleability and ductility are due to the fact that the electrons can slip into new spaces created as the atoms are hammered into new positions. Their lustre is caused by the moving electrons reflecting light.

Metals and their reactivity

The table on the next page sets out how different metals react when heated, which metals react the most and the products produced when the metals are heated.

Important facts about the reactivity series of metals

1. The more reactive the metal, the more stable its compounds.
2. A stable compound is highly unlikely to break or decompose because its bonds are tightly held together.
3. When a metal reacts, it gives up an electron to form ions.
4. Most metals occur naturally as oxides. These metals can be extracted by heating the oxides with a more reactive metal.

Metal	Behaviour	Order of reactivity	Product
Sodium	Catches fire with only a little heating. Burns fiercely with a bright yellow flame.	Most reactive ↑	Sodium peroxide, Na_2O_2, a pale yellow powder
Magnesium	Catches fire easily. Burns with a blinding white flame.		Magnesium oxide, MgO, a white powder
Iron	Does not burn, but the metal glows brightly in O_2 and gives off a yellow spark.		Iron oxide, Fe_3O_2, a black powder
Copper	Does not burn, but a hot metal becomes coated with a black substance.		Copper oxide, CuO, a black powder
Gold	No reaction, no matter how much the metal is heated.	Least reactive	None

Ways of extracting metals

Electrolysis | Electrolysis is used for extracting sodium from rock salt. The rock salt is first melted in a giant steel tank (see Chapter 17), for example:
Sodium chloride → Sodium + Chlorine
$2NaCl(l) → 2Na(l) + Cl_2(g)$

Roasting in air | Some copper is found free in nature, but most occurs as copper(I) sulphide in ore copper pyrites. The copper is extracted by roasting the sulphide in air, for example:
Copper(I) sulphide + Oxygen → Copper + Sulphur dioxide
$Cu_2S(s) + O_2(g) → 2Cu(l) + SO_2(g)$

Heating with carbon monoxide | This method is used for extracting iron from iron ore in a blast furnace (see Chapter 24), for example:
Iron(III) oxide + Carbon monoxide → Iron + Carbon dioxide
$Fe_2O_3(s) + 3CO(g) → 2Fe + 3CO_2(g)$

Questions

1. Metals are good conductors of electricity because:
   A they contain positive and negative ions
   B they have mobile nuclei that are positively charged
   C they have a mobile pool of electrons
   D they have a mobile pool of protons.
2. Which of the following non-metals is a fairly good conductor of electricity?
   A iodine
   B graphite
   C diamond
   D hydrogen
3. A metal will be expected to:
   A give up electrons to a more reactive metal to form a compound
   B lose electrons to a non-metal to form a covalent compound
   C share electrons with a non-metal to form a covalent compound
   D accept electrons from a non-metal to form an ionic compound.
4. Non-metals can:
   I accept electrons from metals to form ionic compounds
   II share electrons with other non-metals to form covalent compounds
   III donate electrons to metals to form ionic compounds.
   A I, II and III   C II and III only
   B I and II only   D I only
5. Non-metallic chlorides will:
   I have low melting points
   II be solids at room temperature
   III be good conductors of electricity.
   A I, II and III   C II and III only
   B I and II only   D I only
6. All metallic oxides:
   A are acidic oxides   C are amphoteric oxides
   B are basic oxides   D will react with acids.
7. Silicon dioxide is insoluble in water but is still classified as an acidic oxide. This is mainly because:
   A it is a non-metallic oxide
   B it has both basic and acidic properties
   C it reacts with alkalis to form salt and water only
   D it does not react with acids.
8. Which of the following metals will readily react with dilute acids?
   I magnesium   II zinc   III lead
   A I, II and III   C II and III only
   B I and II only   D I only
9. Which of the following is a list of metals that will be liquids at 100 °C?
   A mercury, sodium, potassium
   B mercury, sodium, magnesium
   C mercury, sodium, calcium
   D mercury, calcium, magnesium

24 Extraction and uses of metals

Most metals are too reactive to be found free (uncombined) in nature. The metals that are found free in nature are the unreactive ones – copper, silver and gold. All other metals have to be extracted from their compounds. The metallic compound along with other impurities is referred to as the ore of the metal, for example, bauxite is the ore for aluminium, containing aluminium oxide with silicon and iron(III) oxide among the impurities. These metals will be positively charged in their compounds. All extraction processes are therefore reduction processes: $M^{z+} + ze \rightarrow M$ (metal).

Choice of extraction methods

The choice of a method for the extraction of a metal is guided by the position of the metal in the E.C.S. Methods available are (a) electrolysis of aqueous solutions (b) electrolysis of molten compounds (c) reduction of oxides using carbon or carbon monoxide, and (d) displacement of metallic ions using a more electropositive metal.

K
Na
Ca — Extracted by the electrolysis of their molten compounds.
Mg
Al

Zn
Fe — Found mostly as their oxides, carbonates and sulphides. Extracted by the reduction of their oxides using carbon or carbon monoxide.
Pb

Cu
Ag — Found free in nature. Copper is extracted by displacement or by electrolysis of aqueous solution.
Au

The metals from potassium to lead cannot be extracted by electrolysis of their aqueous solutions as hydrogen gas will be produced at the cathode. The metals from potassium to aluminium cannot be extracted by reduction of their oxides by carbon because the oxides are too stable and would require such a high temperature that it would be impracticable and uneconomical.

These metals are also too reactive to be displaced from aqueous solutions. They are therefore extracted by electrolysis of their molten compounds, mainly the chlorides.

Zinc and iron are extracted by reduction of their oxides using carbon and carbon monoxide respectively. This method can be used because the oxides of these metals are not so stable, requiring a lower temperature to reduce them than the metals higher in the E.C.S.

In addition, iron, being a transition metal, has such a high melting point that the temperature required for reduction is practicable.

Extraction of sodium ores: sodium chloride and sodium nitrate

Sodium is extracted by the electrolysis of molten sodium chloride. Calcium chloride is added to lower the melting point to around 600 °C. The electrodes used are a carbon anode and an iron cathode.

Anodic reaction	Cathodic reaction
$2Cl^- \rightarrow Cl_2 + 2e$	$Na^+ + e \rightarrow Na$

Extraction of aluminium ores

- Bauxite (Al_2O_3) $2H_2O$
- Cryolite Na_3AlF_6

The purified bauxite (aluminium oxide) is dissolved in cryolite (itself an aluminium ore).

The cryolite is needed because aluminium oxide has a very high melting point. The energy needed to melt the aluminium oxide without cryolite would have made the process uneconomical.

The electrodes used are a graphite anode and a steel cathode:

At anode: $2O^{2-} \rightarrow O_2 + 4e$
At cathode: $Al^{3+} + 3e \rightarrow Al$

Extraction of iron ores

- Haematite (Fe_2O_3) Magnetite (Fe_3O_4)
- Iron(II) carbonate $(FeCO_3)$

The extraction is carried out in a blast furnace. At the bottom of the furnace, carbon combines with oxygen to form carbon dioxide:

$C(s) + O_2(g) \rightarrow CO_2(g)$

Higher up in the furnace, the carbon dioxide is converted to carbon monoxide as the supply of oxygen is less:

$CO_2(g) + C(s) \rightarrow CO(g)$

Carbon monoxide reduces the iron(III) oxide at a temperature of about 1 000 °C:

$Fe_2O_3(s) + 3CO(g) \rightarrow 2Fe(s) + 3CO_2(g)$

The limestone used decomposes to calcium oxide and carbon dioxide. The calcium oxide removes silica (SiO_2) as calcium silicate which is the slag:

$CaCO_3(s) \rightarrow CaO(s) + CO_2(g)$
$CaO(s) + SiO_2 \rightarrow CaSiO_3(s)$

The iron is heavier than the slag and sinks to the bottom. Both are tapped off as shown in the diagram.

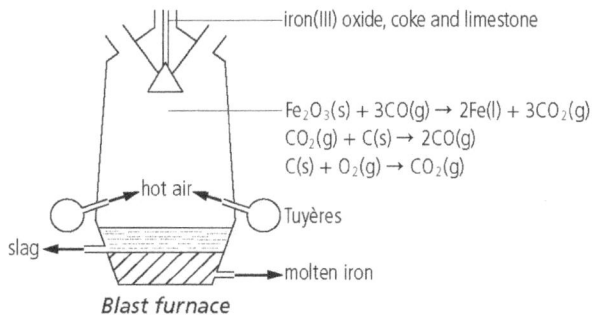

Blast furnace

Uses of metals and their compounds

Sodium

1. Sodium is used in the manufacture of soda and sodium cyanide. The latter is used in the extraction of gold.
2. Sodium chloride is used in the manufacture of sodium hydroxide, chlorine and sodium carbonate.
3. Sodium is used as a coolant in nuclear reactors.
4. Sodium is used as a lead in the manufacture of tetraethyl lead. This is used as an antiknock additive in gasoline.

Iron

1. Iron is used in the form of steel in the construction of buildings and bridges because of its high tensile strength.
2. It is also used in this form to make military vehicles, heavy-duty machinery and stainless steel cutlery.
3. It is used in the form of tin plate in the canning industry.
4. It is used when coated with zinc (galvanised) to make roofing materials. The coating of zinc prevents rusting.
5. Iron is used to manufacture tools.

Aluminium

(Aluminium is protected from corrosion by a protective oxide coating.)

1. Aluminium is used for overhead electrical cable because of its lightness and good electrical conductivity.
2. It is used as an alloy with many metals in aircraft construction because of its lightness yet high tensile strength.
3. It is used to make cooking utensils, being light and a good conductor of heat. It also looks attractive.
4. Aluminium is also used in the manufacture of aluminium paint.

Zinc

1. Zinc is used for galvanising iron to prevent rusting.
2. It is used as one of the electrodes in Leclanché cells.
3. It is also used as an alloy (brass).

Copper

1. Copper is used as electrical cables.
2. It is used as an alloy (bronze, brass) to improve its tensile strength.
3. It is used as an alloy with nickel to make coins.

Mercury and lead are two very toxic metals, causing mercury (Minamata tragedy) and lead poisoning. Zinc is also highly toxic to plants and animals.

Useful effects

Iron is an important constituent of haemoglobin, which is the component of blood that transports oxygen in the blood. Magnesium is an important part of chlorophyll, which is found in green plants.

Questions

1. Iron is extracted using a blast furnace.
   a. Name two iron ores.
   b. Which other raw materials are used in the process?
   c. Explain the chemistry of the process, writing chemical equations for each stage.
   d. Why is this method of extraction used?
   e. Give two uses of iron.
2. Sodium is extracted by the electrolysis of molten sodium chloride.
   a. Name the electrodes used in the process.
   b. Write equations to represent the reactions occurring at the electrodes.
   c. One substance is added to the sodium chloride. Name this substance and explain its use.
   d. Why is sodium not extracted by the electrolysis of aqueous sodium chloride?
   e. Can the metal be extracted by the reduction of its oxide? Explain your answer.
   f. Give two uses of sodium.
3. Aluminium is extracted by the electrolysis of purified bauxite.
   a. What is purified bauxite?
   b. One other substance is used in the extraction. Name this substance and explain its use.
   c. Write the equations for the reactions occurring at the electrodes.
   d. Why is this metal not extracted by the reduction of its oxide using carbon or carbon monoxide?
   e. Give three uses of aluminium relating each use to the properties of the metal.

25 Chemistry of some non-metals

Carbon, sulphur and phosphorus all exhibit **allotropy**, or polymorphism, i.e. they have different forms that are in the same state. The different forms of each element are called **allotropes**.

Allotropes of sulphur

The two main allotropes of sulphur are rhombic (octahedral) and monoclinic sulphur. These two forms are crystalline. Plastic sulphur is an amorphous allotrope.

Preparation of rhombic sulphur

Powdered sulphur is dissolved in carbon disulphide (take care as this solvent is very flammable). The mixture is then filtered through a dry filter paper into a dry beaker. The solution is left to evaporate in a fume cupboard leaving crystals of rhombic sulphur behind.

Preparation of monoclinic sulphur

Some powdered sulphur is placed in an evaporating basin and heated with a low flame until the sulphur melts. More sulphur is added and stirred until it melts. Continue doing this until the evaporating dish is almost filled with molten sulphur. The molten sulphur is allowed to cool until a crust just forms over the surface. At this point a few holes are quickly pierced through the crust and the molten sulphur, from within, is poured out. A knife is used to cut around the crust, exposing needle-shaped crystals of monoclinic sulphur.

Properties of the two allotropes

Rhombic	Monoclinic
Octahedral crystals	Needle-shaped crystal
Density 2.08 g cm^{-3}	Density 1.98 g cm^{-3}
Melting point 114 °C	Melting point 119 °C
Stable at temperature below 96 °C	Stable at temperature above 96 °C

$$\text{rhombic} \underset{}{\overset{96\,°C}{\rightleftharpoons}} \text{monoclinic}$$
transition temperature

Allotropes of carbon

The allotropes of carbon are diamond, graphite and amorphous carbon, which includes charcoal and lampblack. The important properties of graphite and diamond can be found in Chapter 6.

Allotropes of phosphorus

The two allotropes are white (yellow) phosphorus and red phosphorus.

Properties of the two allotropes

White (yellow) phosphorus	Red phosphorus
White solid becoming yellow on exposure to air	Red solid
Density 1.8 g cm^{-3}	Density 2.3 g cm^{-3}
Very poisonous	Non-poisonous
Melting point 44 °C	Sublimes at 400 °C
Readily ignites in air at about 30 °C.	Ignites in air at about 260 °C.
Rapidly oxidised in air at ordinary temperatures.	Is not oxidised at ordinary temperatures.

Uses of some non-metals

Uses of carbon

See Chapter 6.

Uses of sulphur

Sulphur is used (a) in the manufacture of sulphuric acid, (b) in the vulcanisation of rubber, (c) as a fungicide for vines, and (d) in fireworks, dyes and certain medicinal ointments.

Uses of phosphorus

Red phosphorus is used in the match industry and in rat poisons. Compounds of phosphorus are also used as phosphate fertilisers. Phosphorus is the basic material for a wide range of insecticides.

Uses of silicon

This element is mainly used in the production of transistors and microcircuits in the computer industry. As silica, it is used in the manufacture of cement and glass. It is also used to make laboratory crucibles.

Uses of nitrogen

Nitrogen gas is used in the manufacture of ammonia, which is used to make fertilisers. Liquid nitrogen is used as a cooling agent. The gas is very often used where an inert atmosphere is needed, for example in the manufacture of nylon 66.

Some reactions of non-metals

Reactions with oxygen

Most non-metals react with oxygen to form acidic oxides. Phosphorus burns readily in air to form phosphorus(V) oxide, sulphur burns with a blue flame to form sulphur dioxide, and carbon burns to form carbon dioxide. All three are acidic oxides.

$4P(s) + 5O_2(g) \rightarrow P_4O_{10}(s)$
$S(s) + O_2(g) \rightarrow SO_2(g)$
$C(s) + O_2(g) \rightarrow CO_2(g)$

Hydrogen gas burns with a quiet blue flame to form water.

$2H_2(g) + O_2(g) \rightarrow 2H_2O(l)$

Reactions with concentrated acids

Both carbon and sulphur are oxidised by hot concentrated sulphuric and nitric acids.

$C(s) + 2H_2SO_4(l) \rightarrow 2H_2O(l) + 2SO_2(g) + CO_2(g)$
$S(s) + 2H_2SO_4(l) \rightarrow 2H_2O(l) + 3SO_2(g)$
$C(s) + 4HNO_3(l) \rightarrow 2H_2O(l) + 4NO_2(g) + CO_2(g)$
$S(s) + 4HNO_3(l) \rightarrow 2H_2O(l) + 4NO_2(g) + SO_2(g)$

Ammonia

This is a colourless gas with a pungent choking smell. Ammonia is less dense than air and very soluble in water.

Chemical properties of ammonia

Ammonia dissolves in water to give a weak, basic solution that can react with acids to give salts and water.

$NH_4OH(aq) + HCl(aq) \rightarrow NH_4Cl(aq) + H_2O(l)$

Ammonia combines directly with hydrogen chloride to give ammonium chloride.

$NH_3(g) + HCl(g) \rightarrow NH_4Cl(s)$

Ammonia acts as a reducing agent and is able to reduce metal oxides when heated.

$2NH_3(g) + 3CuO(s) \rightarrow 3Cu(s) + N_2(g) + 3H_2O(g)$

Questions

1. Allotropes of an element:
   A are atoms of the element that have the same atomic number but different mass number
   B are forms of the element in different states
   C are different forms of the element with the same melting point
   D are different forms of the element with the same state.

2. What best proves that rhombic and monoclinic sulphur are different forms of the same element?
   A They both burn in air to form sulphur dioxide.
   B They are both yellow in colour.
   C One form can be converted to the other by heating or cooling.
   D Equal masses of each can be converted to the same mass of sulphur dioxide.

3. When carbon is reacted with concentrated sulphuric acid, two gases are formed. Both of these gases will:
   A burn in air with a blue flame
   B turn calcium hydroxide solution cloudy
   C turn blue litmus red
   D decolourise acidified potassium manganate(VII).

4. Phosphorus and sulphur both burn in air to form oxides. Which of the following are properties of these oxides?
   I They are soluble in water.
   II They are acidic to litmus.
   III They are all solids.
   A I, II and III   C II and III only
   B I and II only   D I only

5. Which of the following substances burn with a blue frame?
   I carbon monoxide
   II sulphur
   III hydrogen
   A I, II and III   C II and III only
   B I and II only   D I and III only

6. Which of the following is used in the vulcanisation of rubber?
   A sulphur   C carbon
   B phosphorus   D silicon

7. Phosphorus is an element that exhibits allotropy.
   a What is meant by the term 'allotropy'?
   b Name two allotropes of phosphorus.
   c Give two differences in properties between the allotropes named in b.
   d Give two uses of phosphorus or phosphorus compounds.
   e Two other elements that exhibit allotropy are sulphur and carbon.
      i Name two forms of each of these elements.
      ii For the allotropes named in a, give two differences in properties for each element.
      iii Give one use each of sulphur and carbon.

8. Silicon is an element in Group IV of the periodic table. Its oxide is insoluble in water.
   a The oxide of silicon is commonly called silica. It is classified as an acidic oxide. Give one reason for this classification.
   b Silicon is used in the computer industry. In what form is it mainly used?
   c Laboratory crucibles are made of silica. What property makes silica suitable for this purpose.
   d What other substance, or substances, are used along with silica to make (i) cement (ii) glass?

26 Water

Unique properties of water

Water is a very important substance without which life would be impossible. During winter, ponds freeze from the top, thus insulating the water at the bottom and preventing the entire pond from freezing. This enables fish to live during winter. This pattern of freezing occurs because ice has a lower density than water at 0 °C. Water expands as it cools from 4 °C to 0 °C. The colder water, which has a lower density than water above 4 °C, will rise to the top and so freezing begins.

Water is a polar solvent and can dissolve polar and ionic substances. Plants can therefore absorb salts from aqueous solutions, through the roots. Also, animals can absorb ionic compounds into their bloodstreams from aqueous solutions in their stomachs.

The high specific heat capacity of water enables water to absorb a lot of heat with little change in temperature. This is very important in the temperature regulation of plants and animals. The unusually high boiling point of water, due to strong inter-molecular hydrogen bonds, makes it possible for lakes, rivers and oceans to exist.

Hardness of water

The hardness of water is caused by dissolved calcium and magnesium salts: calcium and magnesium sulphates, and calcium and magnesium chlorides. This prevents the water from forming a lather with soap.

Temporary hardness

Temporary hardness is due to the presence of calcium hydrogen carbonate and magnesium hydrogen carbonate. This type of hardness can be removed by boiling the water. Heat converts the soluble hydrogen carbonates to insoluble carbonates, thus removing the compounds from the solution.

$$Ca(HCO_3)_2(aq) \rightarrow CaCO_3(s) + CO_2(g) + H_2O(l)$$

Permanent hardness

Permanent hardness is hardness that cannot be removed by boiling. It is caused by the presence of dissolved calcium and magnesium sulphates and chlorides. This type of hardness can be removed by adding sodium carbonate crystals. This precipitates the calcium and magnesium in the water as insoluble carbonates.

$$Ca(HCO_3)_2(aq) + Na_2CO_3(s) \rightarrow CaCO_3(s) + 2NaHCO_3(aq)$$

Soap

Soap is the sodium salt of long-chain carboxylic acids such as octadecanoic acid (stearic acid). The chemical formula is $C_{17}H_{35}CO_2H$. Soap can be represented by the formula $C_{17}H_{35}CO_2Na$, an ionic compound. Soap is manufactured by heating vegetable oils or animal fats with caustic soda solution (sodium hydroxide). The reaction is called **saponification**.

Fat + NaOH → Soap + Glycerol

The fat contains esters of long-chain carboxylic acids and glycerol. The esters are hydrolysed by the caustic soda (see Chapter 33). Common salt is often added in the manufacturing process to isolate the soap. The crude soap is purified and then dyes and perfumes are added.

Soap dissolves in water, forming a lather and loosening dirt and oil. The hydrocarbon, non-polar part of the soap, is soluble to grease and fat, allowing them to mix with the polar water.

Effect of hard water on soap

The dissolved calcium salts react with the soap to form an insoluble calcium salt (scum). This prevents the soap from forming a lather, thus neutralising its cleaning properties. Much of the soap is therefore wasted.

Soapless detergents

Soapless detergents are usually manufactured using concentrated sulphuric acid instead of caustic soda. They are preferred to soap because they form no scum with hard water. However, many of the soapless detergents made in the past were non-biodegradable and were responsible for the persistent foam in rivers and streams. The manufacture of this kind of detergent has therefore been discouraged. Many of the detergents found on supermarket shelves today are biodegradable.

Water cycle

The water cycle describes the circulation of water in nature. Water vapour in the air comes from the water in seas, lakes, rivers etc. The vapour rises, cools, and condenses to tiny droplets of water. These float in the sky as clouds, come together and fall as rain. The rain water reaches rivers and seas, and the process is repeated.

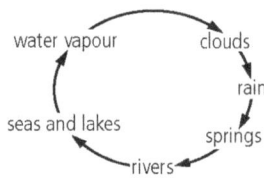

Disadvantages of hard water

Hard water needs more soap than soft water and leaves a messy scum that is difficult to wash out.

Temporary hardness leaves a fur or scale in kettles, hot water pipes, boilers and radiators. This makes them less efficient and can also cause blockage, so the fur has to be removed from time to time.

Ways to soften hard water

Boiling | Boiling removes temporary hardness by the precipitation of the calcium carbonate.

Distilling | Distilling the water gets rid of temporary and permanent hardness. The water is heated and boils off as steam, leaving all the dissolved compounds behind. The steam is then condensed to pure water.

Ion exchangers | Ion exchangers remove temporary and permanent hardness by removing all the calcium and magnesium ions from the water. An ion exchanger is a container full of small beads. These are made of a special plastic called ion exchange resin, which has ions weakly attached to it. When hard water flows through the ion exchanger, the calcium and magnesium ions in the water change places with the sodium ions, and attach themselves to the resin. The sodium ions dissolve in the water.

Questions

1. Which of the following is not a property of water?
   A Contracts as it cools from 4 °C to 0 °C.
   B Has a high specific heat capacity.
   C Is a polar solvent.
   D Has an unusually high boiling point.
2. Which of the following compounds can cause temporary hardness of water?
   I calcium sulphate
   II magnesium hydrogen carbonate
   III calcium hydrogen carbonate
   A I, II and III   C II and III only
   B I and II only   D III only
3. Temporary hardness of water is hardness that:
   A lasts only for a short while
   B is caused by the presence of calcium carbonate
   C can be removed by boiling
   D causes soap to readily form a lather with the water.
4. Which of the following compounds can be used to remove both temporary and permanent hardness?
   A calcium carbonate
   B calcium sulphate
   C sodium hydrogen carbonate
   D sodium carbonate
5. The production of soap from oils and fats is referred to as:
   A neutralisation   C polymerisation
   B esterification   D saponification
6. Removal of any type of hardness depends on the:
   A conversion of an insoluble salt to a soluble one
   B conversion of a soluble salt to an insoluble one
   C thermal decomposition of the compound causing the hardness
   D addition of soluble sodium compound.
7. Soap is a mixture of sodium salts of long-chain carboxylic acids.
   a Name one sodium salt that is present in soap.
   b Soap is prepared by the hydrolysis of animal or vegetable oils and fats.
     i What substance is usually used for the hydrolysis?
     ii What is the process usually called?
     iii Name the substance other than soap that is produced in the process.
   c i What is a soapless detergent?
     ii Give one advantage and one disadvantage that a soapless detergent has compared with soap.
8. Water is a liquid that is essential for life to exist. One of its important properties is that it freezes from the top.
   a i Explain why water freezes from the top.
     ii What implication does this have for aquatic life?
   b Water is described as a polar solvent.
     i Explain what is meant by the term 'polar solvent'.
     ii What kinds of substances can be dissolved by water?
     iii What importance does its solution properties have for plant and animal life?
9. Hardness of water is caused by the presence of dissolved calcium and magnesium salts. Two types of hardness are known: temporary and permanent.
   a i What is meant by the term 'temporary hardness'?
     ii Name two salts that cause temporary hardness.
   b i Explain what is meant by the term 'permanent hardness'?
     ii Name two salts that cause permanent hardness.
     iii State one method used to remove permanent hardness, explaining why the hardness is removed.
   c Hard water reacts with soap to form scum. Explain the formation of the scum.

27 Some industrial processes

Manufacture of sodium hydroxide and chlorine

Sodium hydroxide and chlorine are manufactured by the electrolysis of brine, using a graphite anode and a mercury cathode. The two products are prevented from mixing, and therefore from reacting with each other, by the circulating mercury diaphragm which acts as the cathode. Sodium ions are discharged at the cathode and form sodium amalgam.

$$Na^+(aq) + e \rightarrow Na(s)$$
$$Na + Hg \rightarrow NaHg$$

This amalgam is treated with water in a secondary cell. The products of this process are sodium hydroxide, regenerated mercury and hydrogen.

$$NaHg + H_2O(l) \rightarrow NaOH(aq) + H_2(g) + Hg(l)$$

Chlorine gas is produced at the anode.

$$2Cl^-(aq) \rightarrow Cl_2(g) + 2e$$

Manufacture of sodium carbonate

Sodium carbonate is manufactured by the Solvay process. The raw materials are limestone and sodium chloride. These are cheap and in plentiful supply. The manufacture is done in specially constructed Solvay towers. Concentrated brine, saturated with ammonia flows down the tower, while carbon dioxide is forced up the tower. The towers are equipped with mushroom baffles to slow the flow of the ammoniacal brine and also to present surfaces for the reactions. The reaction taking place is:

$$NaCl(aq) + NH_4OH(aq) + CO_2(g) \rightarrow NaHCO_3(s) + NH_4Cl(aq)$$

The sodium hydrogen carbonate is obtained as a precipitate. It is filtered, washed and heated to give anhydrous sodium carbonate.

$$2NaHCO_3(s) \rightarrow Na_2CO_3(s) + H_2O(l) + CO_2(g)$$

The carbon dioxide which is evolved, is recycled. Ammonium chloride is heated with quicklime obtained from the limestone to produce more ammonia. The only product not fully utilised is the chlorine which is in the form of calcium chloride.

Manufacture of nitric acid

Nitric acid is manufactured by the oxidation of ammonia. The raw materials are air, petroleum and water.

The ammonia is passed with excess air over a platinum (90%) – rhodium (10%) catalyst. The catalyst is heated to red hot at the start of the reaction. The highly exothermic reaction maintains this temperature.

$$4NH_3(g) + 2O_2(g) \rightleftharpoons 4NO(g) + 6H_2(g)$$

The nitrogen monoxide is then cooled and combines with air to form nitrogen dioxide. Nitrogen dioxide is absorbed in hot water in the presence of excess air to give nitric acid.

$$4NO_2(g) + 2H_2O(l) + O_2(g) \rightarrow 4HNO_3(aq)$$

The catalyst is normally in the form of a gauze to increase the reaction surface. The reaction is highly exothermic and so is favoured by low temperature. However, a temperature of about 900 °C is used, as the catalyst needs this temperature to function effectively. A pressure of several atmospheres is used to speed up the rate of reaction.

Manufacture of oxygen

Oxygen is made by the fractional distillation of liquid air. Liquid air is produced by a series of compressions and expansions, and simultaneous cooling. Carbon dioxide and water vapour must be removed as they would solidify and block the tubes through which the air is circulated. Oxygen distils at −183 °C after nitrogen which boils off at −196 °C.

Uses of sodium hydroxide

a Sodium hydroxide is used in the manufacture of soap, rayon and aluminium.
b It is also used in the paper industry.

Uses of sodium carbonate

a Sodium carbonate is used domestically for softening water.
b It is used in the manufacture of glass and also to make water glass (used for preserving eggs).

Uses of ammonia

a Ammonia is used in the manufacture of fertilisers and household cleaners.
b Ammonia is also used in the manufacture of nitric acid.

Uses of nitric acid

a Nitric acid is used in the manufacture of dyes and explosives.
b It is also used in the manufacture of nitrate fertilisers.

Uses of sulphuric acid

a It is used in the manufacture of fertilisers, paints, fibres, for example, rayon, and paper.
b It is used in the manufacture of soaps, detergents and dyes.
c It is used in the manufacture of insecticides, pharmaceuticals and explosives.
d It is also used in the metallurgy and plastic industries.

Questions

1. Which of the following represent the cathodic reaction in the manufacture of sodium hydroxide?
   A $Na^+(aq) + e \rightarrow Na(s)$
   B $Na \rightarrow Na^+(aq) + e$
   C $Na^{2+}(aq) + 2e \rightarrow Na(s)$
   D $Na \rightarrow Na^{2+}(aq) + 2e$
2. Which of the following is used at the cathode in the electrolytic manufacture of sodium hydroxide?
   A carbon   B steel   C platinum   D mercury
3. Which of the following are raw materials used in the manufacture of sodium carbonate?
   I limestone
   II sodium chloride
   III ammonia
   A I, II and III   C II and III only
   B I and II only   D I only
4. In the manufacture of nitric acid, ammonia is oxidised according to the following equation:
   $4NH_3(g) + 5O_2(g) \rightleftharpoons 4NO(g) + 6H_2O(g)$
   In this process, a pressure of a few atmospheres is used because a high pressure will:
   A favour the forward reaction
   B favour the backward reaction
   C lower the temperature
   D speed up the rate of reaction.
5. Which one of the following substances produced in the Solvay process is not utilised?
   A ammonium chloride
   B carbon dioxide
   C sodium hydrogen carbonate
   D calcium chloride
6. Which of the following is **not** a use of nitric acid?
   A in the manufacture of ammonia
   B in the manufacture of dyes
   C in the manufacture of explosives
   D in the manufacture of fertilisers.
7. Sodium hydroxide and chlorine are manufactured by the electrolysis of brine.
   a What is the raw material used in the process?
   b Name the substance used as (i) anode (ii) cathode.
   c Write equations representing the reactions taking place at the (i) anode (ii) cathode.
   d Sodium amalgam, formed at the cathode, is treated with water in a secondary cell. The products are sodium hydroxide, hydrogen and mercury. Write an equation for the reaction.
   e Give two uses each of sodium hydroxide and chlorine.
8. This question concerns the manufacture of sodium carbonate.
   a Name the raw materials used in the process.
   b The Solvay towers used in the manufacture of sodium carbonate are equipped with baffles. Give two reasons for the use of the baffles.
   c Sodium carbonate is obtained by the action of heat on precipitated sodium hydrogen carbonate.
      i Write an equation for this reaction.
      ii Explain how crystals for sodium carbonate can be obtained from the anhydrous sodium carbonate.
   d Suggest a reason why potassium carbonate cannot be manufactured by a similar process.
   e Give two uses of sodium carbonate.
9. Nitric acid is manufactured by the catalytic oxidation of ammonia.
   a What are the raw materials used in the process?
   b Which catalyst is used in the process?
   c The equation for the reaction is:
      $4NH_3(g) + 5O_2(g) \rightarrow 4NO(g) + 6H_2O(g)$
      i What conditions of temperature and pressure will favour the above reaction?
      ii State the conditions actually used, explaining why they are used.
   d Give two uses of nitric acid.
10. Oxygen, with a boiling point of −183 °C, can be separated from liquid air. The other major substance in liquid air is nitrogen which boils at −196 °C.
    a Explain how air is liquefied.
    b Two substances present in the air must first be removed before the air can be liquefied. Name the two substances and explain why they must first be removed.
    c What is the name of the process used to separate oxygen from liquid air.
    d Which gas will boil off first, oxygen or nitrogen?
    e Apart from nitrogen and oxygen, name two gases present in liquid air.
    f Give two uses of oxygen.

28 Preparation and identification of gases

Preparation of gases

Name of gas	Apparatus no.	Reactants and methods	Equation	Drying agent	Uses
Oxygen	I (page 60)	Hydrogen peroxide and manganese(IV) oxide. No heat required.	$2H_2O_2(l) \rightarrow 2H_2O(l) + O_2(g)$	Concentrated H_2SO_4 or anhydrous calcium chloride	As an aid to breathing while diving and in high altitude flying and also for use in hospitals. For the oxy-acetylene flame to weld and cut steel.
Hydrogen	I	Zn, Mg or Fe with dilute sulphuric or hydrochloric acids. No heat required.	$Zn(s) + H_2SO_4(g)$ $\rightarrow ZnSO_4(aq) + H_2(g)$	Concentrated H_2SO_4 or anhydrous calcium chloride	To fill weather balloons. To make margarine. To make synthetic petrol. To make ammonia.
Carbon dioxide	I	Any carbonate and dilute acid except calcium carbonate and dilute H_2SO_4. No heat required.	$CaCO_3(g) + 2HCl(aq)$ $\rightarrow CaCl_2(aq) + H_2O(l) + CO_2(g)$	Concentrated H_2SO_4 or anhydrous calcium chloride	In fire extinguishers. As dry ice as a refrigerant. In the manufacture of soft drinks.
Ammonia	II (page 60)	Any ammonium salt and alkali, for example, ammonium chloride and calcium hydroxide. Heat is required.	$2NH_4Cl(s) + Ca(OH)_2$ $\rightarrow 2NH_3(g) + CaCl_2(g) + 2H_2O(l)$	Calcium oxide (quicklime)	In the manufacture of nitric acid and fertilisers. As a large-scale refrigerant, for example in ships.
Chlorine	III (page 61)	Concentrated hydrochloric acid and (a) manganese(IV) oxide or (b) potassium manganate(VII). Heat is required in (a).	$4HCl(aq) + MnO_2(s)$ $\rightarrow MnCl_2(aq) + 2H_2O(l) + Cl_2(g)$	Concentrated H_2SO_4 or anhydrous calcium chloride	As a bleaching agent and in the manufacture of bleaching agents. To sterilise water in homes and swimming pools. To manufacture organic chemicals.
Chlorine	III	Sodium chloride, manganese(IV) oxide followed by concentrated H_2SO_4. Heat is required.	$NaCl(s) + H_2SO_4$ $\rightarrow HCl(g) + NaHSO_4(s)$ $4HCl(aq) + MnO_2(s)$ $\rightarrow Cl_2(g) + 2H_2O(l) + MnCl_2(aq)$	Concentrated H_2SO_4 or anhydrous calcium chloride	As a bleaching agent and in the manufacture of bleaching agents. To sterilise water in homes and swimming pools. To manufacture organic chemicals.

Identification of gases

Gas	Colour	Odour	Reaction with lighted or glowing splint	Reaction with litmus	Characteristic test
Hydrogen	Colourless	Odourless	Explodes when a lighted splint is applied in the presence of air.	No reaction.	Same as with lighted splint.
Oxygen	Colourless	Odourless	Relights a glowing splint.	No reaction.	Same as with glowing splint.
Carbon dioxide	Colourless	Odourless	Extinguishes a lighted splint.	Turns moist litmus a claret (pale red) colour.	Forms a white precipitate of calcium carbonate with calcium hydroxide solution (lime water).
Ammonia	Colourless	Characteristic choking smell	Extinguishes a lighted splint.	Turns moist litmus blue. It is the only common alkaline gas.	a Litmus test b Dense white fumes with hydrogen chloride gas
Sulphur dioxide	Colourless	Irritating smell	Extinguishes a lighted splint.	Turns moist litmus red.	Decolourises acidified potassium manganese(VII). Turns potassium dichromate (VII) from orange to green.
Hydrogen sulphide	Colourless	Unpleasant smell of a rotten egg	Extinguishes a lighted splint.	Turns moist litmus red.	Turns lead ethanoate (acetate) paper black.
Hydrogen chloride	Colourless	Irritating choking smell	Extinguishes a lighted splint.	Turns moist litmus red.	Gives a white precipitate when a drop of silver nitrate on a glass rod is held in the gas. Gives dense white fumes with ammonia.
Chlorine	Greenish-yellow	Irritating, choking smell, poisonous	Extinguishes a lighted splint.	Bleaches moist litmus.	Same as with litmus.
Nitrogen dioxide	Reddish-brown	Irritating smell, poisonous	Extinguishes a lighted splint.	Turns moist litmus red.	Identified by colour and action on moist litmus.
Water vapour	Colourless	Odourless	Extinguishes a lighted splint.	No reaction.	Turns cobalt(II) chloride paper from blue to pink.

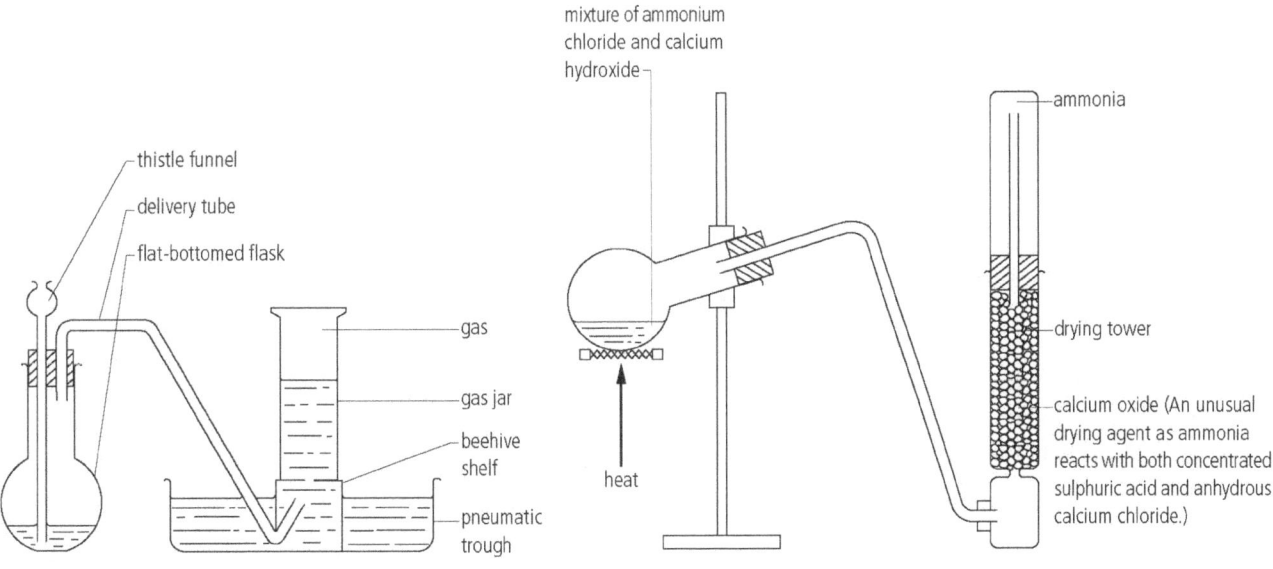

I

II

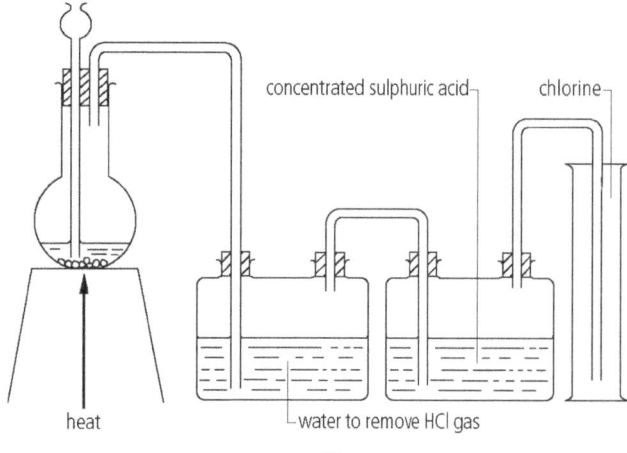
III

Questions

1. Manganese(IV) oxide is used along with hydrogen peroxide in the laboratory preparation of oxygen. In this reaction the manganese(IV) oxide:
   A decomposes to give oxygen gas
   B is used to supplement the hydrogen peroxide
   C is used to speed up the rate of decomposition of hydrogen peroxide
   D is acting as an oxidising agent.

2. Which of the following pairs of substances would you not use to prepare hydrogen gas?
   A sodium and dilute sulphuric acid
   B magnesium and dilute sulphuric acid
   C iron and dilute hydrochloric acid
   D zinc and dilute sulphuric acid

3. Zinc reacts fairly slowly with dilute sulphuric acid. Which of the following substances can be used to speed up the rate of the reaction?
   I copper(II) sulphate
   II copper(II) chloride
   III zinc sulphate
   A I, II and III   C II and III only
   B I and II only   D I only

4. Which of the following pairs of substances cannot be used to prepare carbon dioxide gas?
   A sodium carbonate and dilute hydrochloric acid
   B sodium carbonate and dilute sulphuric acid
   C calcium carbonate and dilute hydrochloric acid
   D calcium carbonate and dilute sulphuric acid

5. Which of the following substances can be used to dry ammonia gas?
   A concentrated sulphuric acid
   B calcium oxide
   C anhydrous calcium chloride
   D copper(II) oxide

6. Manganese(IV) oxide is used with concentrated hydrochloric acid, in the laboratory preparation of chlorine. The manganese(IV) oxide is:
   A an oxidising agent   C a catalyst
   B a reducing agent   D a drying agent.

7. Which of the following best describes oxygen gas?
   A A colourless gas which causes a burning splint to burn brighter.
   B A colourless, odourless gas which allows a lighted splint to continue burning.
   C A colourless gas which relights a glowing splint.
   D A colourless, odourless gas which relights a glowing splint.

8. Sulphur dioxide gas will:
   I   decolourise acidified potassium manganate(VII)
   II turn acidified potassium chromate(VII) from orange to green
   III turn moist blue litmus red.
   A I, II and III   C II and III only
   B I and II only   D I only

9. Which of the following is a list of gases that will turn blue litmus red?
   A carbon dioxide, oxygen, hydrogen
   B carbon dioxide, hydrogen sulphide, oxygen
   C carbon dioxide, nitrogen dioxide, ammonia
   D carbon dioxide, nitrogen dioxide, hydrogen chloride

10. Water vapour will turn anhydrous:
    I   copper(II) sulphate from white to blue
    II cobalt(II) chloride from blue to pink
    III calcium chloride from white to blue.
    A I, II and III   C II and III only
    B I and II only   D I only

11. Choose substances to match these descriptions.
    a Substance A is a black solid that reacts with substance B, a colourless liquid, to give a greenish-yellow gas C.
    b Heat is applied to a mixture of two colourless substances D and E to give an alkaline gas F.
    c A colourless liquid G is added to a blue solid H to produce a gas I that turns limewater cloudy.

12. Ammonia gas can be prepared in the laboratory by the action of heat on a mixture of any ammonium compound and any alkali.
    a Name a pair of substances that can be used in the preparation.
       i Which substance is used to dry ammonia gas?
       ii Explain why this substance is used.
    c How can ammonia gas be identified?
    d The gas is usually collected by upward delivery. This shows that the gas is (i) lighter than air (ii) heavier than air?
    e Give two uses of ammonia gas.

29 Nitrogen cycle, carbon dioxide cycle and pollution

Nitrogen cycle

The diagram below illustrates the nitrogen cycle in which nitrogen is recycled through natural and human-made processes.

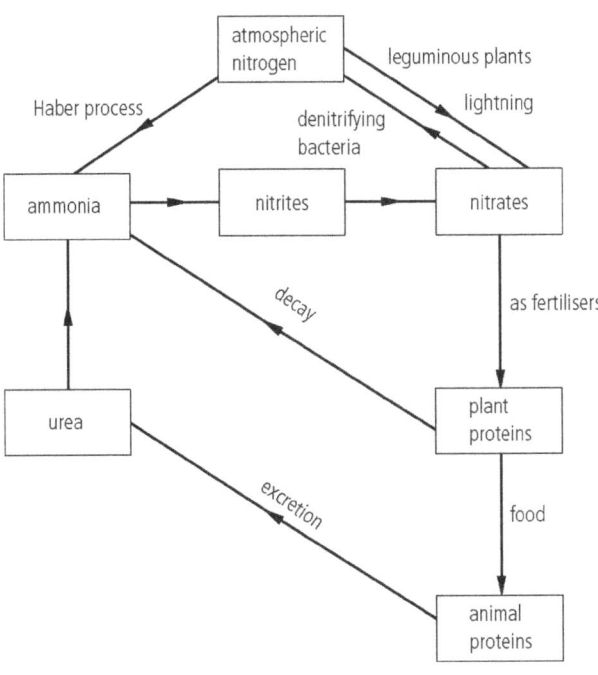

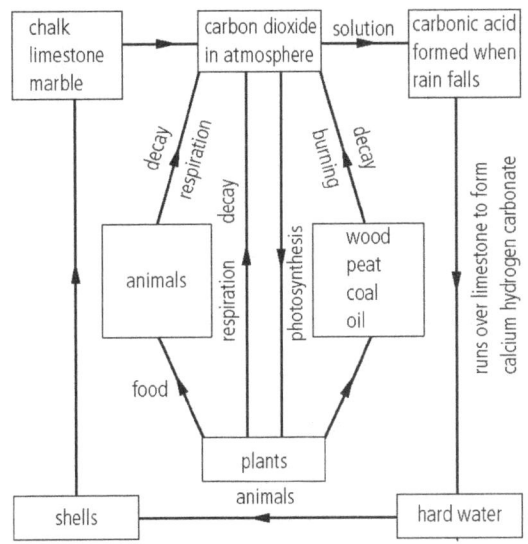

Nitrogen and oxygen are combined by lightning to form nitrogen monoxide, which is eventually converted to nitrates. Bacteria in leguminous plants convert atmospheric nitrogen to nitrates.

Carbon dioxide cycle

This cycle deals with the recycling of carbon dioxide by natural and human-made processes.

Carbon dioxide is added to the atmosphere through:
a the respiration of plants and animals
b the thermal decomposition of calcium carbonate
c the processes of combustion
d fermentation.

Carbon dioxide is removed from the atmosphere by:
a the solution of the gas in water due to rainfall
b photosynthesis.

Environmental effects of some non-metals and their compounds

Carbon monoxide is an impurity found in the atmosphere as a result of incomplete combustion of fuels used in automobiles. It is a poisonous gas and can be fatal if inhaled for a short while in enclosed places, for example a closed garage. Carbon monoxide prevents the blood from transporting oxygen, because the carbon monoxide forms a more stable compound with haemoglobin.

The gas is also present in coal gas. Carbon monoxide is a colourless, odourless gas and is a neutral oxide. It burns in the air with a blue flame to form carbon dioxide.

$$2CO(g) + O_2(g) \rightarrow 2CO_2(g)$$

It is a very good reducing agent, reducing metallic oxides to the metals. For example, it is the effective reducing agents in the blast-furnace production of iron.

Two other pollutants found in the air are sulphur dioxide and hydrogen sulphide. These are largely found in areas where there are coal-burning plants. Sulphur dioxide is an acidic gas and will therefore attack metallic and limestone structures. Hydrogen sulphide readily tarnishes metals such as silver.

Some non-metals and their compounds are, however, useful to living systems, especially to plants. Carbon, phosphorus and nitrogen are a few of the essential non-metals needed by plants. Plants make use of carbon dioxide and water to make food in a process called photosynthesis. Energy from the sun is also used in this process.

Pollution of the atmosphere

Oxides of nitrogen

Nitrogen is released from electric power plants, and is also found in automobile exhaust gases. Sulphur dioxide and the oxides of nitrogen released into the air are eventually converted into sulphur and nitric acids and fall to the ground as **acid rain** or **acid snow**.

Carbon monoxide

Carbon monoxide is a pollution produced by the incomplete combustion of carbon-containing substances such as fossil fuels. It is mainly released into the air from automobile exhausts.

Carbon monoxide produces an odourless and colourless gas. This gas is poisonous and insoluble in water. When it combines with the haemoglobin in the red blood cells, a substance called carboxyhaemoglobin is formed. This reaction is irreversible and it effectively depletes the blood of haemoglobin. As a result, the blood loses much of its ability to carry oxygen and the person dies due to the lack of oxygen.

Other pollution

Apart from carbon monoxide and other monoxides of nitrogen, automobile exhausts also release lead and hydrocarbon (from unburnt fuel) into the air.

Another vehicle pollution is **OZONE**, produced by the action of sunlight on the exhaust gases. Fortunately, strong emission controls for cars are now in effect in many countries of the Caribbean and also in other parts of the world.

Other atmospheric pollutants include fine solid particles from incinerators, and chlorofluorocarbons (CFCs). CFCs are used in refrigeration and as propellants in many aerosol spray cans. CFCs rise into the upper atmosphere where they damage the **ozone layer**.

Questions

1. In the nitrogen cycle, atmospheric nitrogen is converted to:
   I ammonia by the Haber process
   II nitrates by bacteria found in leguminous plants
   III nitrates by lightning.
   A I, II and III   **C** II and III only
   B I and II only   **D** I only

2. Carbon dioxide is returned to the atmosphere by the:
   I process of photosynthesis
   II respiration of living things
   III combustion of fuels.
   A I, II and III   **C** II and III only
   B I and II only   **D** III only

3. Which of the following elements is present in haemoglobin?
   A iron   **B** magnesium   **C** zinc   **D** calcium

4. Which of the following gases is formed as a result of lightning?
   A carbon dioxide   **C** sulphur dioxide
   B carbon monoxide   **D** nitrogen dioxide

5. A gas which is sometime present in air as a pollutant and which causes acid rain is:
   A nitrogen
   B ammonia
   C sulphur dioxide
   D carbon monoxide

6. A gas not found in clean air is:
   A argon
   B oxygen
   C carbon dioxide
   D nitrogen dioxide

7. Which of the following is the correct order in which to describe the oxides: H_2O, CaO, Al_2O_3 and CO_2?
   A neutral, basic, amphoteric, acidic
   B neutral, basic, acidic, acidic
   C neutral, basic, basic, acidic
   D acidic, basic, amphoteric, neutral

8. Carbon monoxide is an impurity found in the earth's atmosphere.
   a What is the chief source of this carbon monoxide?
   b Carbon monoxide is very poisonous. It prevents the blood from transporting oxygen. Explain why this happens.
   c What type of oxide is carbon monoxide?
   d Explain the role of carbon monoxide in the extraction of iron.
   e Name two other pollutants found in the air and state what effect they have on buildings and/or metals.

9. a Name three non-metallic elements that are useful to living systems.
   b Explain the importance of these elements.
   c Name two fertilisers that together contain all the elements named in (a).

10. a Name one gas that is needed by plants for the manufacture of food.
    b Briefly explain how the gas is utilised.
    c Which gas is given off by green plants (i) in sunlight (ii) during the night? Explain.

30 Qualitative analysis

Tests to identify cations

The following table details tests that can be carried out, and the expected observations to identify cations. All of these tests, excluding that for the ammonium ion, must be carried out in aqueous solutions.

Cation	Test	Observation
Calcium (Ca^{2+})	Add aqueous ammonia.	No precipitate obtained with dilute ammonia.
Calcium (Ca^{2+})	Add aqueous sodium hydroxide.	White precipitate, insoluble in excess.
Lead (Pb^{2+})	Add aqueous sodium hydroxide.	White precipitate that is soluble in excess.
Lead (Pb^{2+})	Add aqueous ammonia.	White precipitate that is insoluble in excess.
Lead (Pb^{2+})	Add dilute sulphuric acid.	White precipitate.
Aluminium (Al^{3+})	Add aqueous sodium hydroxide.	White precipitate that is soluble in excess.
Aluminium (Al^{3+})	Add aqueous ammonia.	White precipitate that is insoluble in excess.
Zinc (Zn^{2+})	Add aqueous sodium hydroxide.	White precipitate that is soluble in excess.
Zinc (Zn^{2+})	Add aqueous ammonia.	White precipitate that is soluble in excess.
Copper (Cu^{2+})	Add aqueous sodium hydroxide.	Light-blue precipitate that is insoluble in excess.
Copper (Cu^{2+})	Add aqueous ammonia.	Light-blue precipitate dissolving in excess to give a clear, dark blue solution.
Iron(II) (Fe^{2+})	Add aqueous sodium hydroxide or aqueous ammonia.	Dirty, green precipitate that is insoluble in excess.
Iron(III) (Fe^{3+})	Add aqueous sodium hydroxide or aqueous ammonia.	Reddish-brown precipitate that is insoluble in excess.
Ammonium (NH_4^+)	Add aqueous sodium hydroxide to a sample of the solid, or to its aqueous solution, and warm.	Gas evolved with a characteristic choking smell. The gas will turn moist red litmus blue. The gas is ammonia.

Tests to distinguish between calcium, aluminium, zinc and lead cations

Test	Observation	Ions present
Add aqueous sodium hydroxide.	White precipitate insoluble in excess.	Calcium
	White precipitate soluble in excess.	Aluminium, lead or zinc
Add aqueous ammonia.	White precipitate soluble in excess.	Zinc
	White precipitate insoluble in excess.	Aluminium or lead
Add dilute sulphuric acid or hydrochloric acid.	White precipitate.	Lead
	No precipitate.	Aluminium

Tests to identify anions

These tests can be carried out to identify anions.

Action of heat on substances

A sample of the solid is heated in a test tube.

Observation	Ion present
Carbon dioxide gas evolved.	Carbonate or hydrogen carbonate
Oxygen gas evolved.	Nitrate of sodium or potassium
Nitrogen dioxide and oxygen gases evolved.	Nitrates of metals from calcium to silver in reactivity series
Sulphur dioxide gas evolved.	Sulphite

Action of dilute acid

Add dilute acid to a sample of the substance and test the gas evolved. Warm the mixture if necessary.

Observation	Ion present
Carbon dioxide evolved.	Carbonate or hydrogen carbonate
Sulphur dioxide evolved.	Sulphite
Hydrogen sulphide.	Sulphide

Action of concentrated sulphuric acid

Carry out this test on a sample of the solid in a test tube. The above observations will be made along with the following. (Tests must be carried out in a fume hood.)

Observation	Ion present
Hydrogen chloride evolved.	Chloride
Hydrogen bromide and brown fumes of bromine.	Bromide
Hydrogen iodide evolved and purple vapour of iodine.	Iodide

Action of dilute nitric acid and aqueous silver nitrate, followed by aqueous ammonia

Carry out this test on the aqueous solution of the compound.

Observation	Ion present
White precipitate soluble in aqueous ammonia.	Chloride
Cream precipitate partially soluble in aqueous ammonia.	Bromide
Yellow precipitate almost insoluble in aqueous ammonia.	Iodide

Action of barium nitrate or chloride solution, followed by dilute hydrochloric acid or nitric acid and warming if necessary

Carry out this test on the aqueous solution of the compound.

Observation	Ion present
White precipitate insoluble in acid.	Sulphate
White precipitate dissolving in acid giving carbon dioxide gas.	Carbonate
White precipitate dissolving in acid when warmed to give sulphur dioxide gas.	Sulphite

Action of concentrated sulphuric acid followed by copper turnings

Observation	Ion present
Pale yellow vapour followed by brown fumes of nitrogen dioxide as copper is added.	Nitrate

Questions

1. A sodium hydroxide solution is added to an aqueous calcium salt. What will you observe?
   A No reaction.
   B A white precipitate that dissolves in excess alkali.
   C A white precipitate that will not dissolve in excess alkali.
   D A white precipitate after adding a lot of alkali.

2. Aqueous sodium hydroxide is added to solutions containing lead or aluminium ions. In both cases a white precipitate that dissolves in excess alkali forms. Which of the following aqueous solutions can be used to distinguish between the two ions?
   A dilute sulphuric acid
   B dilute hydrochloric acid
   C sodium sulphate
   D none of the above

3. Which of the following ions will form precipitates that dissolve with aqueous ammonia?
   I copper(II)   II zinc(II)   III iron(II)
   A I, II and III   C II and III only
   B I and II only   D I only

4. Which of the following will not form a precipitate with dilute aqueous ammonia?
   A Ca^{2+} B Cu^{2+} C Fe^{2+} D Pb^{2+}

5. When aqueous barium chloride is added to an aqueous solution, a white precipitate forms. Which of these ions could be present in the solution?
   I Pb^{2+} II SO_3^{2-} III SO_4^{2-}
   A I, II and III   C II and III only
   B I and II only   D III only

6. When a solid, X, was heated, it produced a brown gas which rekindled a glowing splint. X could be:
   A copper(II) sulphate   C sodium nitrate
   B copper(II) nitrate   D potassium nitrate

7. When concentrated sulphuric acid is added to a solid in a test tube, a gas, that gives a white precipitate with aqueous silver nitrate, is evolved. The anion present in the solid could be:
   A Br^- B I^- C Cl^- D SO_3^{2-}

8. Which of the following anions will form a white precipitate with aqueous silver nitrate?
   I Cl^- II CO_3^{2-} III SO_4^{2-}
   A I, II and III   C II and III only
   B I and II only   D I only

31 Alkanes

Carbon forms many compounds with other elements, mainly with hydrogen. The chemistry of these compounds is referred to as organic chemistry. The simplest set of organic compounds are the **alkanes**.

Names	Molecular formula	Melting point (°C)	Boiling point (°C)
Methane	CH_4	−183	−162
Ethane	C_2H_6	−172	−88
Propane	C_3H_8	−187	−42
Butane	C_4H_{10}	−138	0
Pentane	C_5H_{12}	−130	36

Notice that:
a All members of the alkane series conform to a general formula, i.e. C_nH_{2n+2}.
b Each member differs from the next member by a CH_2 unit. Thus molecular mass increases by 14 units as you go from one member to the next.
c Because of the increase in molecular mass, physical properties such as (i) melting points, (ii) boiling points, and (iii) density, increase as the number of carbon atoms in the alkane increases. (Note that the maximum density is about 0.8 g cm^{-3}.)
d All members of the series have similar chemical reactions though they may differ in vigour.
e All members of the series will have general methods of preparation.

The above characteristics are those of a **homologous series** of organic compounds. The alkanes make up such a series and are referred to as **hydrocarbons**. A hydrocarbon is a compound containing carbon and hydrogen *only*. They can also be called hydrides.

Structural formulae of alkanes

Consider the alkane, methane. Its molecular formula is CH_4. This gives the number of atoms of each element in one molecule of the compound, but it does not show how the atoms are bonded to each other.

Carbon has the electronic configuration 2)4. It will therefore exhibit a covalency of 4.

Here is a dot and cross diagram for methane:

```
            H           X H electron
            X           O C electron
            O
      H X O C O X H
            O
            X
            H
```

This shows carbon sharing four pairs of electrons with four hydrogen atoms, forming four covalent bonds. In organic chemistry, each covalent bond is represented by a dash —. Thus, methane can be represented as:

```
            H
            |
      H —— C —— H
            |
            H
```

The above formula is known as the **structural formula** of methane.

Notice that: a Each carbon atom forms four covalent bonds.
b Carbon is always bonded to carbon in the higher order alkanes

Draw structural formulae for ethane, propane, butane and pentane.

Note: Although it may appear from the structural formula that methane is a flat molecule with H—C—H bond angles of 90%, *this is not so*.
In a methane molecule, the C—H bonds are directed towards the corners of a tetrahedron. The shape of the methane molecule is therefore tetrahedral with all the H—C—H bond angles equal to 109.5°. Two of the bonds will be in one plane, with a third behind the plane and the fourth in front of it.

Cycloalkanes (C_nH_{2n})

There are also some ring compounds called cycloalkanes. The first is a three-membered ring of carbon atoms.

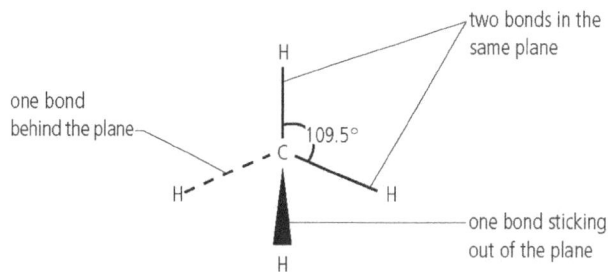
cyclopropane

They have the general formula C_nH_{2n}. Their chemical reactions are similar to the open-chained alkanes.

Isomerism

Consider the following structures numbered I and II.

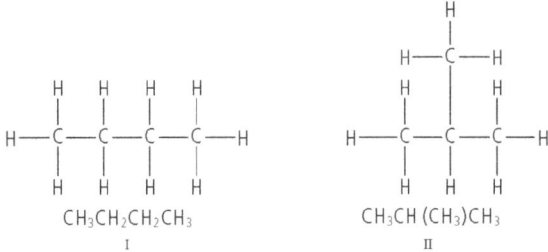

Structures I and II have the same molecular formula, but different structural formulae. They are called **isomers**. Isomers are compounds that have the same molecular formula, but different structural formulae.

Note that structure III is the same as structure I above. It is only drawn differently on the paper.

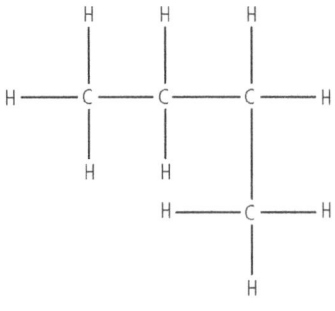

The best way to work out whether given structures are isomers is to write out the groups as shown above, i.e. $CH_3CH_2CH_2CH_3$, etc. If the groupings are the same, then the structures are the same.

Draw isomers of pentane, C_6H_{14}.

Chemistry of the alkanes

The sources of alkanes are petroleum and natural gas.

Laboratory preparation of methane

Methane can be prepared by the action of heat on a mixture of sodium ethanoate and soda-lime (an impure form of sodium hydroxide).

$$CH_3COONa(s) + NaOH(s) \rightarrow CH_4(g) + Na_2CO_3(s)$$

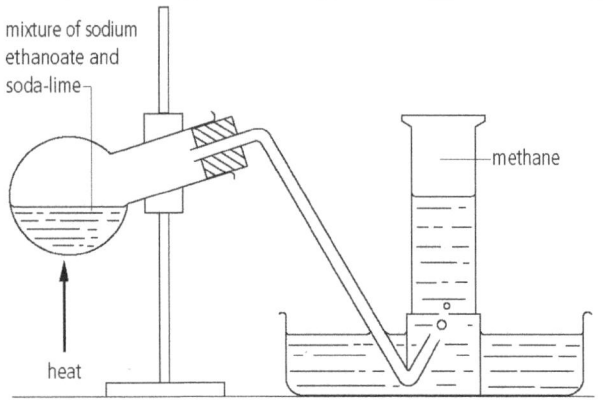

Reactions of alkanes

1. Alkanes burn readily in air, or oxygen, to produce carbon dioxide, water and, more importantly, heat. For example:
   $$CH_4(g) + 2O_2(g) \rightarrow CO_2(g) + 2H_2O(g) + \text{heat}$$
   Because the reaction is highly exothermic, alkanes can be used as fuels. They also cause little pollution as the products, carbon dioxide and water, are normally present in the air. However, the incomplete combustion of gasoline in car engines can lead to the production of carbon monoxide, a very toxic gas.

2. Alkanes also react readily with chlorine in sunlight.
   $$CH_4(g) + Cl_2(g) \xrightarrow{\text{sunlight or UV light}} CH_3Cl(g) + HCl(g)$$

   This reaction is called a **substitution reaction** as one chlorine atom replaces a hydrogen atom. The reaction can go on until all the hydrogen atoms are replaced.
   $$CH_3Cl(g) + Cl_2(g) \rightarrow CH_2Cl_2(l) + HCl(g)$$
   $$CH_2Cl_2(l) + Cl_2(g) \rightarrow CHCl_3(l) + HCl(g)$$
   $$CHCl_3(l) + Cl_2(g) \rightarrow CCl_4(l) + HCl(g)$$

$CHCl_3$ (trichloromethane) is commonly known as chloroform, and CCl_4 (tetrachloromethane) as carbon tetrachloride.

Other halogens can also substitute in an alkane but not with the same vigour or extent as chlorine does, for example:
$$C_2H_6(g) + Br_2(g) \rightarrow C_2H_5Br(g) + HBr(g)$$

The bromine will be decolourised but the reaction will only proceed in ultraviolet light or at high temperatures.

Gasoline and natural gas

Petroleum and the accompanying natural gas are natural sources of alkanes. Natural gas contains mainly methane, and smaller amounts of ethane, propane and butane. The propane and butane are mostly liquefied together and put in cylinders under pressure. The main uses of these gases are as fuels, since they burn in air to produce carbon dioxide, water and heat, i.e. the reactions are highly exothermic. For example:

$$C_xH_y + \left(x + \frac{y}{4}\right) O_2(g) \rightarrow xCO_2(g) + \frac{y}{2} H_2O(g) + \text{heat}$$

Petroleum or crude oil was formed when small marine animals and plants were deposited and buried in the sea millions of years ago. There these animals and plants decayed to crude oil.

Petroleum is fractionally distilled to separate it into different mixtures of hydrocarbons which boil within certain ranges.

Some of the fractions obtained are:

Temperature °C	Fraction
50–175	Gasoline
175–250	Naphtha
250–350	Gas oil
350–400	Heavy oil (fuel oil)

Laboratory distillation of crude oil

A sample of crude oil can be distilled in the laboratory using the following apparatus.

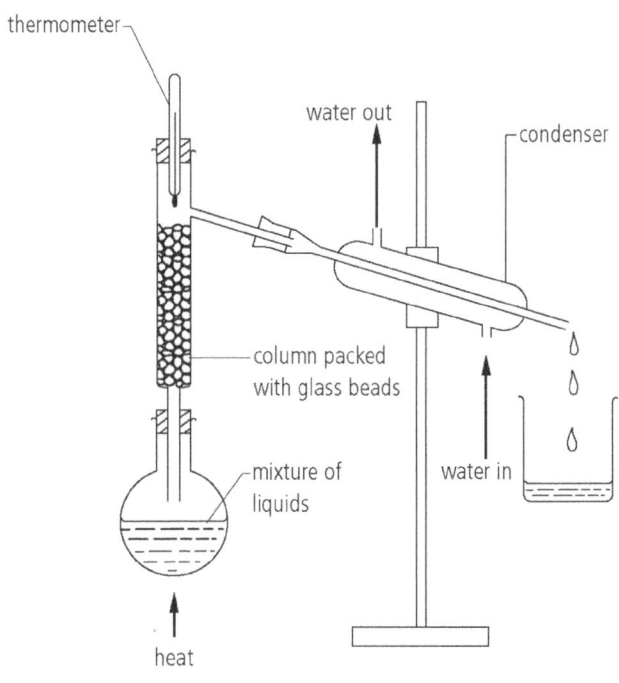

Four fractions can be collected at these temperatures:

Temperature °C	Fraction
25–110	Gasoline
110–180	Naphtha
150–260	Kerosene
260–300	Light gas oil

The heavy oils will be left in the flask.

The uses of alkanes

Alkanes are used as fuels. They burn with clean flames to produce energy in many exothermic reactions. Alkanes can be used as solvents. Many medicinal products and ointments use solid alkanes. They can also be used as lubricants. Waxes and lubricants contain a high percentage of alkanes. Alkanes are used in the making of methane which is used as a source of hydrogen in the production of ammonia. The table in the next column sets out the differences between alkanes and alkenes. For more about alkenes, see Chapter 32.

Test	Alkanes' reactions	Alkenes' reactions
Addition of Br_2 gas	No reaction.	Rapid decolourisation of bromine from red-brown to colourless.
Combustion	Burn with clean flames.	Burn with smoky flames.
Addition of (H^+/$KMnO_4$)	No reaction.	Rapid decolourisation of $KMnO_4$ from purple to colourless.

Questions

1. The members of a homologous series will all have:
   A similar boiling points
   B the same density
   C similar chemical properties
   D the same chemical formula.
2. A hydrocarbon can be described as:
   I a compound containing carbon and hydrogen
   II a compound containing carbon and hydrogen only
   III a hydride.
   A I, II and III   C II and III only
   B I and II only   D II only
3. The structural formula of a hydrocarbon is a formula:
   A showing the shape of the molecule
   B giving the ratio of carbon to hydrogen atoms
   C showing how the atoms are bonded together
   D giving the number of carbon and hydrogen atoms only.
4. The type of reactions that alkanes undergo can be described as:
   A addition   C reduction
   B polymerisation   D substitution.
5. Which of the following are possible products when methane reacts with chlorine in ultraviolet light?
   I CH_3Cl II CH_2Cl_2 III $CHCl_3$
   A I, II and III   C II and III only
   B I and II only   D I only
6. The process of refining crude oil is called:
   A simple distillation   C cracking
   B fractional distillation D dehydration.
7. a Give the names and formulae of the first five alkanes.
   b What trend is observed in the melting points of the hydrocarbons as the series is descended?
   c Choose one member of the series and state what is formed when it reacts with chlorine and the conditions for the reaction. What kind of reaction is this?
   d Draw isomers of the hydrocarbon, pentane.

32 Alkenes

The set of alkenes is another homologous series of hydrocarbons. The general formula is C_nH_{2n}. The first five members are as follows:

Name	Molecular formula
Ethene	C_2H_4
Propene	C_3H_6
Butene	C_4H_8
Pentene	C_5H_{10}
Hexene	C_6H_{12}

Structural formulae of alkenes

Consider ethene, C_2H_4. An electron dot formula to satisfy the octet rule would be as follows:

The alkenes are characterised by a double covalent bond between one pair of carbon atoms. One of these bonds is weaker than the other and is responsible for the kind of chemical reactions of alkenes. Propene can be represented by:

These hydrocarbons are said to be **unsaturated hydrocarbons**, i.e. all the carbons in the alkenes are not fully bonded to hydrogen atoms. The alkanes are referred to as saturated hydrocarbons because the carbon atoms have the maximum number of hydrogen atoms they can accommodate.

Industrial source of ethene

Ethene is obtained industrially as a by-product when the longer-chained alkanes are subjected to **cracking**. Cracking is a process where the alkanes in the gas-oil fraction are heated under pressure in the absence of air to break them down into alkenes in the petrol range.

The reason for doing this is because petrol is in far greater demand than gas oil. There is more gas oil available than the quantity required to satisfy demands.

Laboratory preparation of ethene

Ethene can be prepared in the laboratory by the dehydration of ethanol, C_2H_5OH.
$$C_2H_5OH(l) - H_2O(l) \rightarrow C_2H_4(g)$$

The dehydration can be carried out as follows:
a By using concentrated sulphuric acid.
b By using concentrated sulphuric acid and ethanol in a 2 : 1 ratio. The mixture is heated to about 180 °C. Ethene can be collected over water.
c The dehydration can also be carried out in the following apparatus.

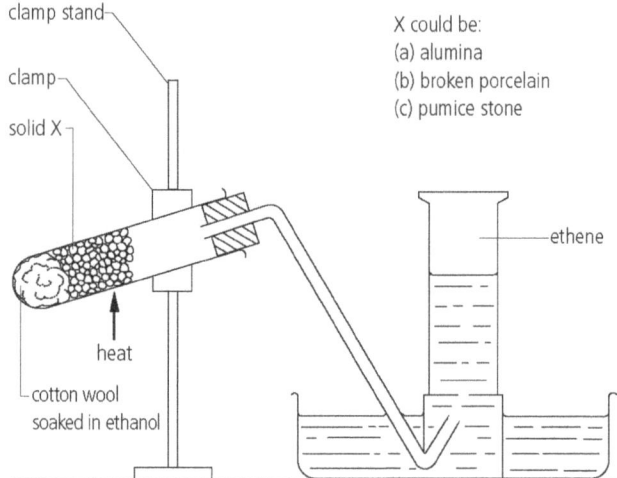

The solid X is heated strongly, occasionally heating the wool for a few seconds. The ethanol is thermally decomposed to ethene:
$$C_2H_5OH(g) \rightarrow C_2H_4(g) + H_2O(g)$$

Properties of ethene

Combustion

Ethene burns in air to produce carbon dioxide and water. The flame is yellow and produces a lot more soot than the corresponding alkane. This is because the alkenes have a higher carbon to hydrogen ratio.
$$C_2H_4(g) + 2CO_2(g) \rightarrow 2CO_2(g) + 2H_2O(g)$$

Addition reactions

The typical reactions of alkenes are **addition reactions**. The alkenes all have a double covalent bond between two carbon atoms. One of these bonds is weaker than the other and will be easily broken when the alkene is attacked by some reagents. This leads to the formation of a *single product*. This is a characteristic of an *addition reaction*, for example:

$$H_2C=CH_2 + X-Y \longrightarrow H_2C(X)-CH_2(Y)$$

As can be seen, addition takes place on both carbon atoms each side of the double bond.

Decolourisation reactions

$$H_2C=CH_2 + Br_2 \xrightarrow[\text{room temperature}]{\text{in CCl}_4} H_2C(Br)-CH_2(Br)$$

The colour of the bromine is destroyed. This reaction can be used to distinguish between a saturated hydrocarbon and an unsaturated one. A saturated hydrocarbon does not decolourise bromine at room temperature.

$$H_2C=CH_2 + Cl_2 \xrightarrow{\text{room temperature}} H_2C(Cl)-CH_2(Cl)$$

Alkenes are used as the starting materials to produce substances such as polythene, polyvinyl chloride and solvents. This is because the double bond in the alkenes makes them much more reactive than the alkanes.

If ethene is passed through acidified aqueous potassium manganate(VII) the latter is decolourised. This can also be used to distinguish between saturated and unsaturated hydrocarbons. The former do not react with potassium manganate(VII).

Hydrogenation

$$H_2C=CH_2 + H_2 \xrightarrow[\text{heat}]{\text{Ni or Pt as catalyst,}} H_3C-CH_3$$

ethene (alkane) → ethane (alkane)

Hydrogenation is also used to convert unsaturated oils to fats which are used in the manufacture of margarine.

Hydration | Ethene can be made to react with steam to produce ethanol. This reaction is used industrially to produce ethanol from ethene.

$$C_2H_4(g) + H_2O(g) \rightarrow C_2H_5OH(l)$$

Questions

1. Which of the following is an alkene?
   A CH_2 **B** C_2H_2 **C** C_2H_4 **D** C_2H_6
2. The typical reaction of alkenes is:
   A substitution   **C** dehydration
   B addition   **D** combustion.
3. Samples of pentane and pentene are both burnt in air. The flame produced by pentene is more sooty than that produced by pentane. This is because:
   A pentane has less carbon atoms than pentene
   B pentane is an alkane but pentene is an alkene
   C pentene has a higher carbon to hydrogen ratio than pentane
   D pentane produces carbon dioxide and water only when it is burnt in air.
4. Which of the following are manufactured from unsaturated compounds?
   I polythene
   II ethanol
   III polyvinyl chloride
   A I, II and III   **C** II and III only
   B I and II only   **D** I only
5. Alkenes can be converted to alkanes by the addition of hydrogen. This reaction is used in the manufacture of:
   A petrol from gas oil
   B ethane from ethene
   C margarine from vegetable oils
   D soap from oils and fats.
6. A colourless neutral gas decolourises acidified potassium manganate(VII) solution. This gas is:
   A ethane   **C** sulphur dioxide
   B ethene   **D** hydrogen sulphide.
7. a Give the names and formulae of the first five alkenes.
   b Why are they referred to as unsaturated hydrocarbons?
   c State what type of reaction they undergo and explain why they react in this way.
   d How is the first member obtained industrially? Give two industrial uses of it.
8. a Describe two ways in which ethene can be obtained in the laboratory from ethanol.
   b Ethene can react with (i) hydrogen and (ii) bromine. In each case, state the conditions for the reactions, write the equations for the reactions and state one use of the reaction in industry or in the laboratory.

33 Alcohols

The alcohols make up another homologous series of organic compounds and have the general formula $C_nH_{2n+1}OH$.

The first five members which are all liquids are:

Name	Formula
Methanol	CH_3OH
Ethanol	C_2H_5OH
Propanol	C_3H_7OH
Butanol	C_4H_9OH
Pentanol	$C_5H_{11}OH$

Structural formulae of alcohols

There is only one structural formula for ethanol (C_2H_5OH):

Propanol has two structural formulae:

Propan-1-ol or 1-propanol

Propan-2-ol or 2-propanol

All the other members, with a greater number of carbon atoms than propanol, will have more than one structural formula and will therefore demonstrate **isomerism**.

Some uses of ethanol

Ethanol is being used more and more as an additive to petrol. It is mixed with petrol to form gasohol which is used in motor cars. It is also used as a solvent for many substances in industry, for example in pharmaceuticals.

The breathalyser test is used to detect alcohol in the breath of motorists. If the person has been drinking, the orange chromate(VI) in the breathalyser is reduced to a green colour by the ethanol.

Manufacture of ethanol

Ethanol is manufactured by using an enzyme to ferment a carbohydrate. In the Caribbean, cane sugar, present in molasses, is the carbohydrate used.

Yeast is mixed with the molasses and left to ferment. One of the enzymes in yeast is zymase. This converts the sugar to ethanol and carbon dioxide. The enzyme can continue to convert the sugar to ethanol until the ethanol concentration is about 14–15%. This concentration of alcohol kills the enzyme and prevents further action. The 'wash' obtained is then distilled to give a greater concentration of alcohol. Wine is obtained from the fermentation of grapes, beer from the fermentation of malt, and cider from the fermentation of apples.

Reactions of ethanol

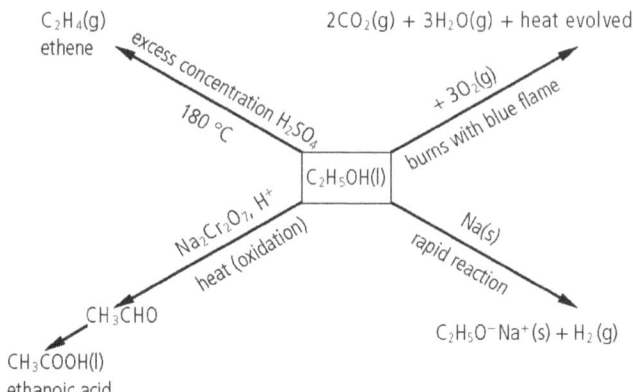

Preparation of ethanoic acid from ethanol

Ethanoic acid is prepared by the oxidation of ethanol. The oxidising agent usually chosen is sodium chromate(VI) in the presence of concentrated sulphuric acid. The mixture must be heated under reflux, i.e. with a condenser placed vertically. The preparation can be conveniently carried out in a 'quick-fit' piece of apparatus. (Care must be taken.) Potassium chromate(VI) is reduced from orange to green. An aldehyde is the first product which must then be refluxed to give ethanoic acid.

The first product of the oxidation is ethanol which is then further oxidised to ethanoic acid:

$CH_3CH_2OH(l) \rightarrow CH_3CHO(g) + 2H^+(aq) + 2e$
$CH_3CHO(g) + H_2O(l) \rightarrow CH_3COOH(aq) + 2H^+ + 2e$

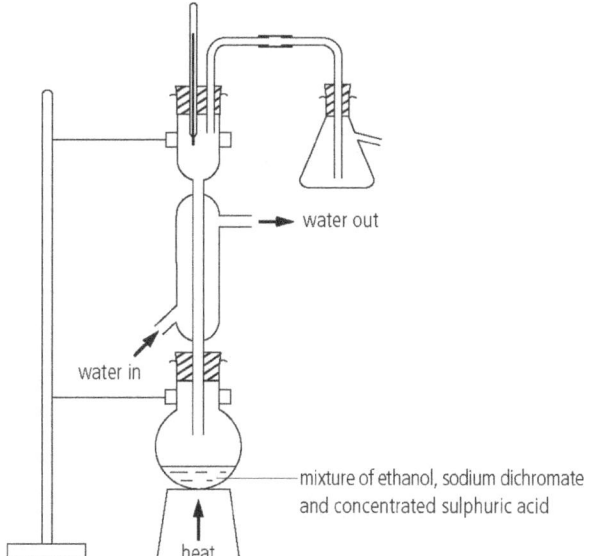

Reactions of ethanoic acid

Ethanoic acid is a weak monobasic acid and will therefore react as a dilute acid in a similar way to hydrochloric and other acids. It will therefore:
a liberate hydrogen from the reactive metals
b liberate carbon dioxide from carbonate
c neutralise hydroxide and basic oxides.

All these reactions would be less vigorous than with the strong mineral acids.

Esterification

Carboxylic acids react with alcohols in the presence of concentrated sulphuric acids as catalyst, to give esters and water.

$CH_3COOH(l) + C_2H_5OH \quad \text{Conc. } H_2SO_4 \ldots$
ethanoic acid   ethanol
$\longrightarrow CH_3COOC_2H_5(l) + H_2O(l)$
ethyl ethanoate
(an ester)

In this reaction, the molecules of water are formed by the combination of hydrogen from the alcohol and OH from the acid.

Esters are sweet-smelling substances present in fruits. They are also present in fats as glycerides. They can be used to make cosmetics, soap and clothing (polyesters).

Hydrolysis of esters

Hydrolysis is basically the reaction with water. The hydrolysis is usually carried out in an alkaline or acid medium.

Acid hydrolysis of the esters gives the carboxylic acid and alcohol that formed the ester, for example:

$CH_3CO_2C_2H_5(l) + H_2O(l) \xrightarrow{H^+} CH_3COOH(aq) + C_2H_5OH(l)$

Alkaline hydrolysis yields the alcohol and the salt of the acid:

$CH_3CO_2C_2H_5(l) + H_2O(l) \xrightarrow{OH^-} CH_3COOO^-(aq) + C_2H_5OH(l)$

This reaction is used in the manufacture of soap. Animal fats or vegetable oils are hydrolysed using caustic soda to give soap. The process is called **saponification**.

Fat or oil + NaOH → Soap + Glycerol
               caustic soda   an alcohol

Manufacture of sugar

In the Caribbean, sugar is extracted from sugar cane. The chart below is an outline of the process generally used to produce sugar.

Flow chart of sugar production

Milk of lime is added to raise the pH. It also acts as a flux by reacting with phosphate, and helps settle solid matter.

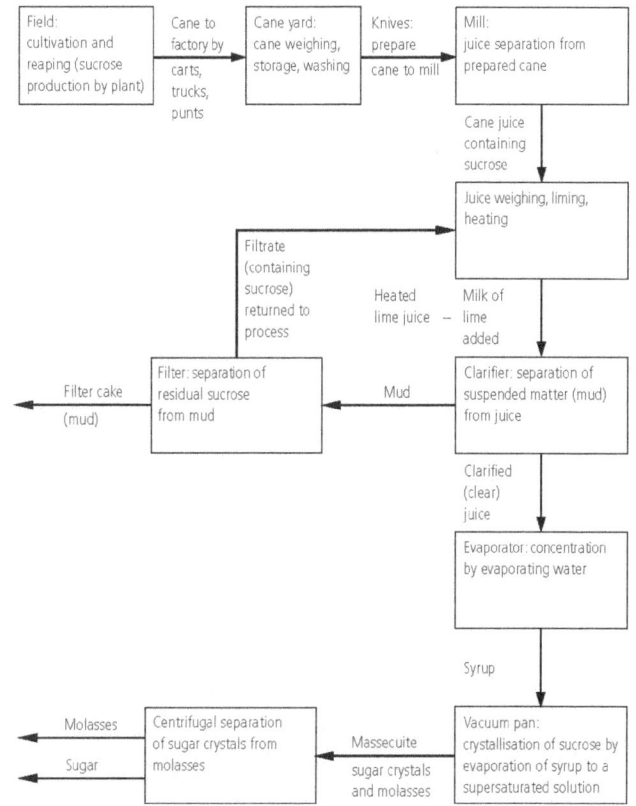

Questions

1. Which of the following substances is an alcohol?
   A CH_3COOH
   B $C_2H_5C = O$
   $\quad\quad\quad\;\;|$
   $\quad\quad\quad\;OH$
   C $CH_3CH(OH)CH_3$
   D CH_3OCH_3

2. Which of the following gases is produced during the fermentation process?
   A oxygen
   B carbon dioxide
   C carbon monoxide
   D hydrogen

3. During the fermentation process, the wash contains about 14% ethanol. Greater concentrations of ethanol can be obtained from the wash by:
   A evaporation
   B filtering then evaporating
   C decantation
   D fractional distillation.

4. Ethene can be obtained from ethanol by reacting with concentrated sulphuric acid. This process can be described as one of:
   A dehydration
   B reduction
   C oxidation
   D addition.

5. Which of the following pieces of apparatus can be used to produce ethanoic acid from ethanol?

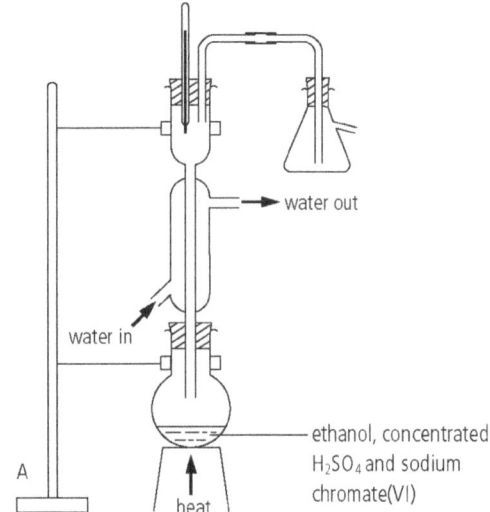

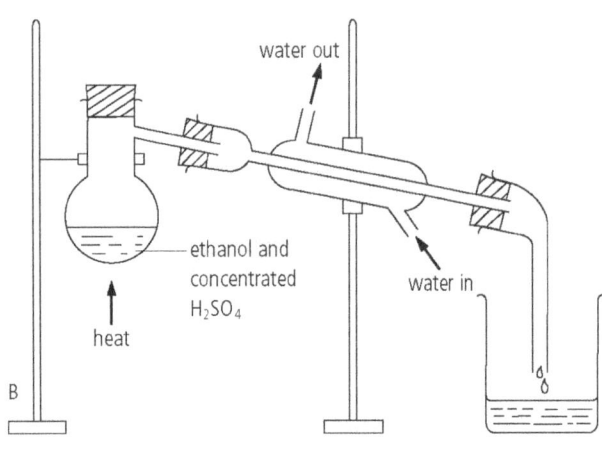

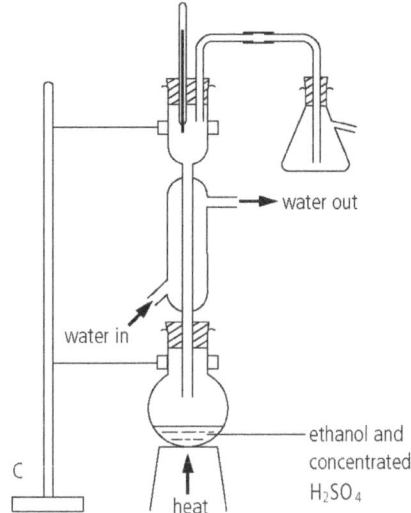

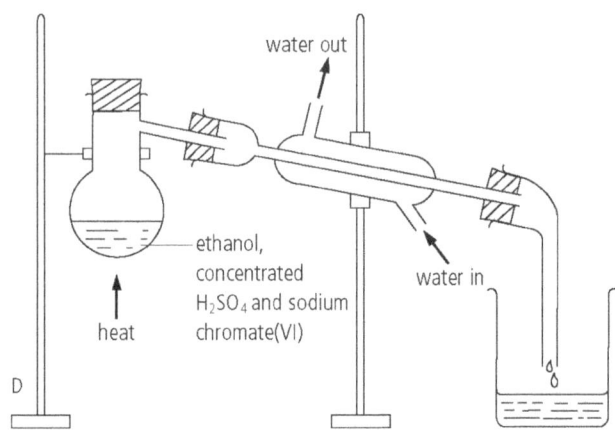

6. Which of the following substances will not react with ethanoic acid?
   A magnesium
   B copper
   C copper(II) carbonate
   D copper(II) oxide

7. The compound formed when ethanoic acid is reacted with methanol is:
   A $CH_3COO_2H_5$
   B $C_2H_5COOCH_3$
   C $CH_2H_5COOCH_3$
   D $C_2H_5COOC_2H_5$

8. Describe the manufacture of sucrose, explaining each step of the manufacturing process as fully as you can.

9. Describe an experiment you have carried out to manufacture a sample of soap. What is the name given to this process?

10. Draw the structural formulae of pentanol.

11. Describe one method used in the Caribbean to manufacture ethanol. Choose three reactions of ethanol and describe what would be observed when these reactions take place.

12. What substance is used in the breathalyser test? Describe the chemical action taking place in the breathalyser when a motorist, who has had some alcohol to drink, blows into it.

34 Natural and synthetic macromolecules

Synthetic macromolecules

Polythene

Polythene is an example of an **addition polymer**. A polymer is a long-chain, high-molecular weight compound formed from a monomer (a small molecule). Polythene is an addition polymer because it is made as a result of an addition reaction between ethene molecules.

$$3n\ H_2C=CH_2 \xrightarrow[\text{pressure and heat}]{\text{trace of oxygen}} (\sim CH_2-CH_2-CH_2\sim)_n$$
polymer ($n \approx 300$)

In addition polymerisation, the polymer is the only product.

monomer A ⟶ —A—A—A—A—A—A— polymer
(the only product)

Polystyrene

Another example of addition polymerisation is the formation of polystyrene (polyphenylethene).

$$3n\ H_2C=CH(C_6H_5) \xrightarrow{\text{heat}} (\sim H_2C-CH(C_6H_5)-CH_2-CH(C_6H_5)-CH_2-CH(C_6H_5)\sim)_n$$
monomer → polymer ($n \approx 5000$)

Terylene

Terylene is referred to as a **condensation polymer** formed by condensation reactions. Two monomers react to give the condensation polymer and a small molecule (usually water). The monomers have *two* functional groups each:

monomer A + monomer B → condensation polymer + small molecule

Substances used in the manufacture of terylene are:
ethane-1,2-diol and 1,4-benzene dicarboxylic acid

HOC_2H_4OH — two alcohol groups represented as $HO-\square-OH$

$HOOC-C_6H_4-COOH$ — two acid groups represented as $HO-C(=O)-\text{▨}-C(=O)-OH$

through a series of esterification reactions

$HO-\square-O-C(=O)-\text{▨}-C(=O)-O-\square-O-C(=O)-\text{▨}-C(=O)-OH + 3H_2O$
ester linkage

The reaction continues until the high molecular mass polymer is formed.

Nylon

Nylon is also a condensation polymer.

monomers: 1,6-diaminohexane   hexanedioic acid

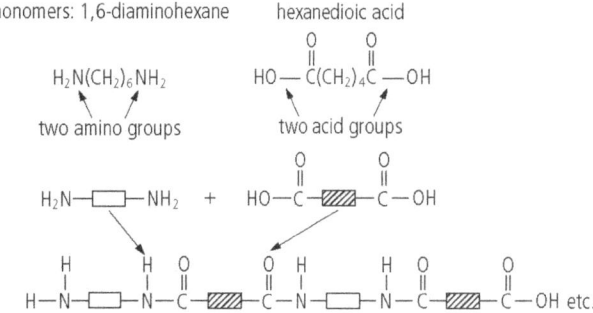

two amino groups   two acid groups

The $\underset{\ \ \ \ C=O}{N-H}$ linkage is called a peptide (amide) linkage. The four macromolecules above are synthetic or human-made and have important uses.

Uses of synthetic macromolecules

Polythene

Polythene is used as wrapping material. It is also used for making cold-water pipes, ropes and twines. High-density polythene is used for making milk crates and bottles.

Polystyrene

Polystyrene is used as a packaging material and as an insulator. It is also used for making plastic toys.

Terylene and nylon

Terylene and nylon are used to make clothing. Nylon is also used to make ropes, brushes, carpets and 'fur' fabric.

Natural macromolecules

Proteins

Proteins are made up of amino acids linked together by peptide linkages. Amino acids contain both amino (NH_2) and carboxyl (COOH) groups.

A typical amino acid can be represented as:

$$H_2N-\underset{H}{\overset{R}{C}}-\overset{O}{\underset{}{C}}-OH$$

R could be H or any alkyl group.

When two amino acids react, the product is called a dipeptide. Three amino acids linked together is called a tripetide. Four or more amino acids together form a polypeptide. A polypeptide that has a molecular weight of about 6 000 or more is called a protein.

amino acid + amino acid → a dipeptide

proteins possess the same kind of linkages as nylon

peptide or amide linkage

When proteins are hydrolysed, for example when treated with dilute acids or when digested, they are converted to the amino acids that they were made from. In the body, the amino acids are transported to where they are needed and re-synthesised to proteins to form new tissues. The individual amino acids can be separated and identified by paper chromatography. The amino acids are identified by using known amino acids as reference when the chromatography is being done.

Fats

Fats are mainly esters of long-chain carboxylic acids, for example, propane-1,2,3-triol (glycerol) and octadecanoic acid (stearic acid), $C_{17}H_{35}COOH$. The linkages are ester linkages like those found in terylene. Hydrolysis of fats produces soap and detergents (see Chapter 30).

Carbohydrates

Carbohydrates are essentially many sugar units linked together by oxygen atoms. They are condensation polymers. A glucose molecule can be represented as: $HOC_6H_{10}O_4OH(C_6H_{12}O_6)$ or HO—☐—OH

Condensation reactions can lead to the kind of structure shown below:

HO—☐—O—☐—O—☐—O—☐—OH

This polymer is called starch which can contain more than 1 000 glucose residues $(C_6H_{10}O_5)$.

Other well-known carbohydrates are: fructose $(C_6H_{12}O_6)$, obtained from fruits; sucrose $(C_{12}H_{22}O_{11})$ (cane and beet sugar) and cellulose.

Cellulose is found in wood, paper, cotton and linen. The filter paper used in the laboratory is a pure form of cellulose.

Hydrolysis of carbohydrates yields the simple sugars that they were made from. These sugars can be separated and identified by paper chromatography.

Identification of glucose (a monomer) and starch (a polymer)

Glucose produces a red precipitate of copper(I) oxide when warmed with Fehling's solution.

Starch forms a blue-black colouration when reacted with iodine solution.

Uses of carbohydrates

Carbohydrates are used in the manufacture of sweets, paper and clothing (cotton and linen).

Hydrolysis of carbohydrates yields the simple sugars that they were made from. These sugars can be separated and identified by paper chromatography.

Polymers

Polymer are covalent molecular compounds in which the molecules are very large (called macromolecules) and are made up of large numbers of smaller repeating units or molecules linked together. There may be several thousand repeating units in a polymer molecule.

These small units from which polymers are made, are called **monomers**. The properties of polymers will depend largely on the size of their molecules. Polymers are grouped into two groups, namely:
1. synthetic polymers
2. natural polymers.

Synthetic polymers are formed by either addition polymerisation or condensation polymerisation.

Addition polymerisation occurs when monomers containing double bonds are combined, for example the formation of polythene from ethene.

$nCH_2 = CH_2 \rightarrow (CH_2CH_2)n$
ethene   polythene

This reaction requires heating at high pressure. Oxygen peroxide is added as the initiator for the reaction above.

Condensation polymerisation

This occurs when a simple molecule (such as H_2O or HCl) is eliminated between pairs of monomers. This process continues between many pairs of monomers to form a chain of alternating units, for example the formation of nylon.

The monomers that assist in the formation of nylon are 1,6-diamonohexane and hexanedioyl dichloride. The combination takes place through the elimination of a molecule of HCl between each pair of monomers. This table shows the polymers, monomers and their uses.

Polymers	Monomers	Uses
Polythene	Ethene	Manufacture of plastic bags, water pipes, film, containers, etc.
Polychloroethene	Chloroethene	Manufacture of toys, water piping and upholstery.
Nylon	1,6-diamino-hexane and hexanedioyl-dichloride	Manufacture of carpets, pantyhose, clothing, parachutes, bearings, etc.
PET, terylene or dacron	Ethane-1, 2-diol and Benzene-1, 4-dicarboxylic acid	Manufacture of blouses, tyres, cords, video tapes, bottles, etc.

Questions

1. Which of the following is an addition polymer?
   A polythene
   B terylene
   C glucose
   D nylon
2. Which of the following is the monomer used in the production of polystyrene?
   A $H_2C=CHCH_3$
   B $H_2C=CHC_2H_5$
   C $H_2C=CHC_6H_5$
   D $H_2C=CH_2$
3. Terylene can best be described as:
   A a macromolecule
   B a natural macromolecule
   C a condensation polymer
   D an addition polymer.
4. Terylene is formed by the polymerisation of an:
   A alkene
   B alcohol and an acid
   C amino compound and an acid
   D amino compound and alcohol.
5. Which of the following substances has the same type of linkage as that found in nylon?
   A fats
   B carbohydrates
   C terylene
   D proteins
6. a Name two addition and two condensation polymers.
   b Give a use of each of the polymers named in (a).
   c Give the names and formulae of the monomers for each of the polymers named in (a).
   d Explain the difference between a condensation and an addition polymer.
7. a Name three natural macromolecules.
   b Draw block diagrams to represent these macromolecules.
   c Name the linkages present in these macromolecules.
   d State how each macromolecule can be hydrolysed, and name the products of hydrolysis.

Answers to questions

Chapter 1
2 10^{10}
3 a $0.05\ cm^3$
   b $5 \times 10^{-6}\ cm^3$
   c $3.33 \times 10^{-7}\ cm$
4 Level at X will rise.
5 a **C** and **D**
   b **B**
   c **D**
   d **C**
   e **A, E, F**
   f **B**

Chapter 3
1 i 20p, 20e, 20n
   ii 18p, 18e, 22n
   iii 1p, 1e
   iv 1p, 1e, 1n
2 X = electrons
   Y = neutrons
   Z = protons
3 protons = 48
   electrons = 48, 48
4 a **A, C, B, D**
   b 48
   c 2)8)7
   d **E**
5 **A**
6 **A**
7 **B**
8 **B**
9 **D**
10 **D**

Chapter 4
2 a $Li^+_2 O^{2-}$
   b $Na^+_2 S^{2-}$
   c $Mg^{2+} O^{2-}$
   d $Ca^{2+} Cl^-_2$
3 **A** 17 17 18 A^-
   B 20 20 18 B^{2+}
   C 16 16 18 C^{2-}
   D 1 1 0 D^+
   E 8 8 10 E^{2-}
6 **C**
7 **B**

Chapter 5
1 i CCl_4
   ii NH_3
   iii SCl_2
2 a ionic
   b covalent
   c covalent
   d covalent
   e covalent
   f ionic
   g none
   h none

3 a covalent
   b ionic
   c covalent
   d covalent
   e ionic
4 **C**
5 **B**

Chapter 6
1 **B**
2 **A**
3 **C**
4 **B**
7 i **B**
   ii **C**
   iii **A**

Chapter 7
4 Li and Mg
   Na and Ca
   Be and Al
5 a chlorine
   b potassium
   c oxygen
   d calcium
6 **B**
7 **B**
8 **D**

Chapter 8
1 **F**
2 **B**
3 **B**
4 **G, H, I**
5 a **G**
   b **I**
6 **K**
7 **J**
8 **K**
9 **A**
10 **F**
11 **K**
12 **L**
13 a **C, H, J**
   b **M**
15 **D**
16 **B**
17 **C**

Chapter 9
1 **C**
2 **C**
3 **B**
4 **A**
5 **C**

Chapter 10
1 **A**
2 **C**
3 **A**
4 **D**

Chapter 11
1 **A**
2 **C**
3 **D**
4 **B**
5 **C**
6 **D**
7 a 2 g
   b 32 g
   c 36.5 g
   d 34 g
   e 20 g
   f 44 g
8 a 0.25
   b 0.5
   c 2
   d 1
   e 0.25
   f 0.5

Chapter 12
1 **C**
2 **B**
3 **D**
4 **D**
5 **B**
6 **A**
7 **A**
8 **B**
9 **C**
10 **B**
11 a i 0.64 g
        ii 0.04
    b 0.02
    c 2
    d MO_2
12 a 0.001
    b 0.001
    c i 0.1
       ii 3.55 g
    d i 2.30 g
       ii 0.1
    e 1
    f NaCl

Chapter 13
1 **A**
2 **C**
3 **D**
4 **B**
5 **D**
6 **A**   7 **C**
8 g 0.0943 M

Chapter 14
1 0.0800 M
2 a 0.0417
   b 4.087
3 0.0500 M
4 a 0.0625
   b 6.63

5 2
6 1
7 133, Cs

Chapter 15
3 a +4
   b +6
   c +4
   d −3
   e +4
   f +1
   g +5
   h +7
   i +2
   j +3
4 **C**
5 **B**
6 **D**
7 **D**
8 **B**
9 **B**
10 **C**

Chapter 16
1 **C**
2 **D**
3 **D**
4 **C**
5 **C**
6 **A**
7 **C**
8 **B**
9 **A**
10 **D**
11 **C**
12 **D**
13 **B**
14 **D**

Chapter 17
1 **C**
2 **B**
3 **C**
4 **B**
5 **A**
6 **C**

Chapter 18
1 **D**
2 **C**
3 **B**
4 **A**
5 **B**
6 **D**
7 **C**
8 **B**
9 **A**   10 **C**
11 a i 1 930 C
       ii 0.02
    d i 120 cm^3
       ii 240 cm^3

12 a i 965 C
       ii 0.01
    c i 120 cm^3
       ii 120 cm^3
13 a 0.0640 g
    b 0.216 g
    c 0.080 g
    d 0.010 g

Chapter 20
1 **A**
2 **B**
3 **A**
4 **B**
5 **C**
6 **B**
7 b 0.050 M
   c 2 730 J
   d −54.6 kJ

Chapter 21
1 **C**
2 **D**
3 **A**
4 **A**
5 **B**
6 **B**
7 **A**
8 **B**
9 **B**
10 **B**

Chapter 22
1 **B**
2 **C**
3 **D**

Chapter 23
1 **C**
2 **B**
3 **B**
4 **B**
5 **D**
6 **D**
7 **C**
8 **B**
9 **A**
10 **C**

Chapter 25
1 **D**
2 **D**
3 **C**
4 **B**
5 **A**
6 **A**

Chapter 26
1 **A**
2 **C**
3 **C**

4 D
5 D
6 B

Chapter 27
1 A
2 D
3 B
4 A
5 D
6 A

Chapter 28
1 C
2 A
3 B
4 D
5 B
6 A
7 D
8 A
9 D
10 B

Chapter 29
1 A
2 C
3 A
4 D
5 C
6 D
7 A

Chapter 30
1 C
2 A, B, C
3 B
4 A
5 A
6 B
7 C
8 A

Chapter 31
1 C
2 C
3 C
4 D
5 A
6 B

Chapter 32
1 C
2 B
3 C
4 A
5 C
6 B

Chapter 33
1 C
2 B
3 D
4 C
5 A
6 B
7 C

Chapter 34
1 A
2 C
3 C
4 B
5 D

Appendix: Measurement

Accuracy and precision of measurements

Scientists perform a number of measurements in the laboratory. It is important to ensure that measurements are very accurate. An accurate measurement is one that is very close to the true or accepted measurement. The greater the precision of the measurement, the greater the chance of the measurement being accurate. For example, if a balance is calibrated to the nearest gram, then the measurement of an object can be estimated to the nearest tenth of a gram. If the balance is calibrated to the nearest tenth of a gram, the measurement can be estimated to the nearest hundredth of a gram. A measurement of 54.25 g is more precise than a measurement of 54.2 g.

Scientists also make multiple measurements to ensure accuracy. A set of measurements that are close to each other is said to have very good precision. Measurements of 54.25 g, 54.24 g and 54.254 g have very good precision. If the accepted value of the object's mass is 54.24 g then the measurements are also very accurate. A measurement of 53.25 g will be inaccurate. Measurements of 53.24 g, 53.23 g and 53.25 g for the same object show very good precision, but poor accuracy. Measurements of 53.25 g, 52.45 g and 51.35 g are inaccurate and show poor precision.

Significant figures

When scientists take measurements, it is important that the measured quantities must be reported with a last digit that is estimated. If a balance is calibrated to the nearest tenth of a gram, the measurement must be reported to the nearest hundredth of a gram. The hundredth digit is estimated, as the balance is not calibrated to measure the hundredth place. A measurement of 54.23 g has three measurements that are known for sure and a final digit (3) that is estimated. All these digits in a measurement are called significant figures.

Significant figures in a measurement contain all the digits that are known (measured by the instrument) plus a final digit that is estimated. In the above measurement the 5, 4 and 2 are known or measured, but the 3 is estimated.

There are rules that allow you to decide how many significant figures a measurement contains. This is very important as it allows you to know the precision of the instrument used to make the measurement. If a measurement of 10.15 cm is reported, then you know that the ruler used to make the measurement is calibrated to the tenth place because the hundredth digit is estimated.

Here is a list of rules that will help you.
1. All non-zero digits in a measurement are significant, for example, 135 cm has three significant figures.
2. The following rules are used for measurements with zeros:
    a. Leading zeros (zeros before non-zero digits) are not significant, for example, 0.00056 g has two significant figures. The zeros are merely place holders.
    b. Captive zeros (between non-zero digits) are always significant, for example, 503 cm has three significant figures and 0.005607 kg has four significant figures.
    c. Trailing zeros (zeros at the right end of a measurement) are only significant when the measurement has a decimal, for example, 5 600 g has two significant figures whereas 56.00 g has four significant figures.

Significant figures in calculations

A scientist cannot report the result of a calculation where the result is greater than the precision of the measurements that were used in the calculation. Therefore:

- In **multiplication** and **division**, the answer must contain the same number of significant figures as the measurement with the **fewest** significant figures. For example: If a rectangle has a length of 10.14 cm and a width of 8.37 cm and we are measuring the area of the rectangle, then the calculator will show an answer of 84.**8**718 cm². However, the answer must contain the same number of significant figures as the measurement with the fewest significant figures. This measurement is 8.37 cm, which has three significant figures. The answer is therefore 84.9 cm² (the bold **8** is rounded up to 9 as the next digit, 7, is greater than 5).
- In **addition** and **subtraction**, the answer must have the same degree of precision (decimal places) as the **least** precise measurement. For example:
19.5 cm + 11.24 cm = 30.74 cm, but the answer must be reported as 30.7 cm as the measurement 19.5 cm is the less precise measurement.

    In the same way, 110 g + 15.45 g = 125.45 g must be reported as 130 g and not as 1**2**5.45 as 110 g is precise to the nearest ten and the answer must therefore be rounded to the nearest ten (the bold **2** is therefore rounded to 3, as the next digit is 5).